THE JOY OF
doing nothing

THE JOY OF
doing nothing

A real-life guide to stepping back, slowing down,
and creating a simpler, joy-filled life

....

RACHEL JONAT

Adams Media
New York London Toronto Sydney New Delhi

Adams Media
An Imprint of Simon & Schuster, Inc.
57 Littlefield Street
Avon, Massachusetts 02322

First Adams Media hardcover edition DECEMBER 2017

ADAMS MEDIA and colophon are trademarks of Simon and Schuster.

For information about special discounts for bulk purchases, please contact Simon & Schuster Special Sales at 1-866-506-1949 or business@simonandschuster.com.

The Simon & Schuster Speakers Bureau can bring authors to your live event. For more information or to book an event contact the Simon & Schuster Speakers Bureau at 1-866-248-3049 or visit our website at www.simonspeakers.com.

Interior design by Michelle Kelly

Manufactured in the United States of America

10 9 8 7 6 5 4 3 2 1

Library of Congress Cataloging-in-Publication Data has been applied for.

ISBN 978-1-5072-0495-5
ISBN 978-1-5072-0496-2 (ebook)

Dedication

For Chris, my favorite person to do nothing with.

Contents

Introduction

6:15 a.m. Your alarm goes off, and you slowly wake to the warm comfort of your bed. Your cat is curled up on the pillow next to you, and you take some moments to scratch her behind the ears, enjoying the deep purr of satisfaction she gives in response to your touch. There's no rush to get out of bed because you've given yourself plenty of time to work through your morning routine. You snuggle back in for another ten minutes and simply listen to the rustle of a light wind in the trees outside your window. When you feel ready to leave your bed, you head to the bathroom for a hot shower to start your day.

. . .

Does this morning scene sound relaxing and amazing? Does it also sound very far from what you currently experience on a daily basis? Finding time to do nothing is an easy and incredibly powerful way to lower your stress, increase your happiness, and enjoy your life.

Just as your body needs rest, so does your mind. We need quiet. We need an opportunity to think of nothing at all. It is restorative and improves your health and overall well-being. It's something you deserve after all your hard work.

Doing nothing can awaken you or it can relax you. Doing nothing can be both a tool to slow down and a tool to make the rest of our time more productive, energizing, and rewarding. Creating these pockets of well-deserved white space in your day gives you an opportunity to relax, de-stress, and appreciate the people and things around you.

If you've ever felt guilty for doing nothing, for "wasting" a Saturday afternoon or for your secret Thursday evening ritual of doing nothing, this book will give you all the reasons you need to joyfully embrace your unscheduled time.

And yes, doing nothing is *joyful*. You will enjoy your life more when you make doing nothing a part of it. The trees really will seem greener, you'll notice the beauty of a building you walk by daily for the first time, and the simple pleasures of life will fill you with contentment. You're going to see the beauty and possibility in a twelve-minute wait for your take-out order. There is so much joy in your daily life that doing nothing will unlock and open you to. You'll see the wonder all around you when you make the time to do nothing.

Doing nothing sounds almost too easy. Turn and stare at your shoes for a few seconds right now—boom, you're making it happen. But so many of us can't find or make the time for this essential component of a healthy life. This book will show you how to incorporate doing nothing into your daily life in a way that's meaningful to you and works with your schedule. After all, everyone is busy. But no matter how much you have on your plate, you'll find easy-to-implement suggestions in this book for reclaiming bits of time throughout your day for doing nothing.

We will examine several areas—Family and Friends, Work, Home, and Other Activities (such as hobbies)—and give you tools for finding the quiet in each of them. Throughout the book, you'll find three "levels" of doing nothing (light, medium, and deep) so you can scale your approach appropriately to your lifestyle. Along the way, you'll learn dozens of real-life ways to create time and space for that most luxurious of activities: doing nothing.

Excited? Great. Now go stare at that water stain on your ceiling that looks like a Buddha for ten minutes and then we'll get started.

The Philosophy of Doing Nothing

Time is the most valuable thing a man can spend.
—Theophrastus, Greek Philosopher

Time: The Ultimate Luxury

Doing nothing is a luxurious type of self-care. When we think about luxury or riches, we often gravitate to the material: cars, home, clothing. But time is the ultimate luxury. Time can't be bought in a store, and it's one of the most sought-after commodities of modern life. Everyone wants more time these days. When you take the time to do nothing, you prioritize self-care and realign your time usage with your values. It's a well-deserved way to recharge after all of your hard work.

When you take the time to do nothing, you prioritize self-care and realign your time usage with your values.

If you prioritize this type of self-care, you'll find out what's important to you. Material goods, shopping, and working harder and longer hours to earn more money and buy more stuff are unfulfilling pursuits. Spend more, make more, buy more, and want more; it's an endless cycle of chasing after things to find happiness. When you hit the pause button and refresh your mind and body with doing nothing, you'll find clarity about what truly brings you meaning and happiness in life.

Restore Yourself with Doing Nothing

To do nothing is to immerse yourself in activities that allow you to rest, replenish, and have fun. This is not a call to laziness but rather an intentional, calm, and proactive effort to save space and time in your life just for yourself. Let yourself do nothing—it is, in fact, sweet and restful time that you need.

As you make the choice to do nothing—for ten minutes, for an hour, for a whole afternoon—you are resisting the pervasive call to be constantly busy, overscheduled, and stressed. You are resting your brain and your body. You are making a conscious decision to put your well-being ahead of mental busyness.

Doing nothing is also a secret path to contentment and productivity. Taking these moments for yourself not only pays you back immediately with a positive and relaxed state of mind, but it also gives you long-term benefits in many areas of your life.

Be More Content

To put it simply, you will enjoy your life more when you make doing nothing a part of it. There is so much beauty in your daily life that doing nothing will show you.

- **You're a happier and less stressed employee, friend, partner, mother, father, sister, brother.** You aren't distracted when talking to people, and you can fully engage with them. That break to do nothing is a reset button and a release. You let the daily and long-term worries and stress go when you actively claim time for yourself. You feel lighter.
- **You enjoy the simple pleasures in your life more.** You are much more aware of all those small but beautiful daily joys.
- **You are grateful.** Fewer distractions allow you to really appreciate all that you have.
- **You find a new perspective.** You see the good in your day ahead of, and in spite of, any bad. The glass really is half full. The usual delays in life like traffic, or someone being late for a meeting, are no longer irritations but rather opportunities. Those delays are now minutes you can take for yourself.

Be More Productive

While it may seem counterintuitive, taking breaks to do nothing actually makes you more productive in the long run.

- **You tackle those hard tasks with ease.** The break to do nothing puts you in a positive feedback loop: less stress, more focus, more energy. You dive into your work without distraction because you took that replenishing break to do nothing. It's suddenly easy to knock out those tough tasks.

- **Your goals sharpen.** What you really want to spend your time on—work, activities, people—becomes clear. You're able to keep all the good stuff and let the rest fall away.

- **New opportunities present themselves to you.** This less stressed, more aware, and engaged you attracts new ideas, people, activities, and work. The universe responds to your openness, your engagement, and your positivity.

- **You embrace and excel at things you once thought out of reach.** Fear of failure is replaced with excitement to try new things. You have the motivation, the focus, and the resolve to take on those things that once scared you.

- **Obstacles and worries disappear.** Obstacles become smaller when we spend time doing nothing. That issue you've been fretting over, the one that's made it hard to fall asleep the last few nights, becomes smaller as you take an hour to yourself to actively not think about it. You're able to off-load the worry and stress of it. Doing nothing cuts out all the distractions so you can see your worries for what they are: things that haven't happened and might never happen.

- **Solutions appear.** You reconnect with your locus of control when you set aside time to do nothing. Realizing you're in control empowers you to find solutions to your problems.

The Health Benefits of Doing Nothing

If all of those amazing reasons weren't enough to convince you, here's another: it's good for your mental and physical health. When we make a habit of doing nothing, as when we make a habit of flossing, our body and mind thank us for it. This habit of doing nothing provides both immediate improvements—less stress, more clarity, a refreshed and relaxed mind—as well as many long-term physical and mental health benefits. Make doing nothing a priority not just for fun but for a break—for a way to channel creativity or to unload some stress as part of your general wellness plan.

Reduce Stress

Deep relaxation exercises like doing nothing can combat stress. That's important because, according to the National Institutes of Health, chronic stress has been linked to tumor development, heart disease, ulcers, and lung ailments. Some studies estimate that as many as 75 to 90 percent of doctor's office visits are for stress-related conditions and complaints! There are many ways to incorporate stress-reducing habits into your life, and doing nothing is an easy way to start.

Fight Disease

We often think of ensuring good health by doing things: exercising, eating nutrient-dense food, getting our teeth cleaned, etc. But relaxing and doing nothing can also be a part of your health and wellness plan. A 2013 Harvard study compared the active disease-fighting genes in people who practiced relaxation exercises and those who did not. People who have practiced relaxation exercises like deep breathing and yoga on a long-term basis have far more active disease-fighting genes than those who don't practice any relaxation exercises. Even better news: the study found that you can switch disease-fighting genes back on in just eight weeks by practicing relaxation exercises regularly. Relaxation can calm you inside and out—but it can also activate important healing mechanisms in the process!

Improve Digestion

General health also gets a boost when you practice relaxation techniques like doing nothing. According to Mayo Clinic research, practicing relaxation even helps with digestion and maintaining normal blood sugar levels.

Avoid Mental and Physical Exhaustion

Taking short breaks to do nothing prevents stress from accumulating. If your life is very stressful, your sympathetic nervous system, the one responsible for your fight-or-flight reaction, may be working overtime. Being in this heightened state on a consistent basis can lead to emotional burnout and exhaustion. Doing nothing is a way to give your sympathetic nervous system a break and let that stress melt away.

Prioritize Your Health

When you take the time to do nothing, to deeply relax and disconnect from any stress or distraction, you are doing good for your mental and physical health. You are making wellness a priority. You are making yourself a priority. This one simple and easy act is giving back to you exponentially. Another way it gives back: you're more present and connected after a break during which you do nothing.

How Do You Do Nothing?

What defines a do-nothing activity?

- Your brain should be in idle mode, and you should feel relaxed and peaceful.
- It should feel easy to walk away from the activity.
- Physical intensity should be very low or nonexistent.
- Your mind and body should move and work with little effort.
- It should also be fun! This isn't a chore or obligation.

Doing nothing is a sweet little luxury you give yourself. You can define your own parameters for what "nothing" looks like in your life. Don't burden yourself with judging your joyful do-nothing activities. This is all about being in the moment. Live in that space and time you have made for yourself and don't compare it to something else you have done, to a friend's result, or what else you could have used that time for. Simply let it happen. Enjoy the act of doing and being rather than comparing the activity to anything. This can be an incredibly hard concept to actualize for those people who are wired to constantly analyze, judge, and grade themselves. If you are one of those people, you'll need to be gentle on yourself as you learn new habits. If you find it hard to enjoy some nonproductive activities a few times a week, you probably need to do nothing more often. The more wound up, over-stimulated, and overscheduled you are, the harder it is to slip into a blissful state of nothingness.

How Often Should You Do Nothing?

If you normally keep a relatively relaxed schedule, you can dive right in to doing nothing. Just start replacing some of your more casual activities or downtime with doing nothing: turn off your phone and let your mind and body relax into a sweet state of nothingness.

If you love being busy and find it hard to relax or "turn off," it's best to start slowly incorporating windows of do-nothing time. You'll find the biggest benefit to doing nothing at the start of your day. If it's all you have time for, spend ten minutes most mornings doing nothing before your day commences. It will pay you back many times over with better focus and a more relaxed attitude. Below are some guidelines for achieving different intensity levels to help you get started.

- **Light:** Find fifteen minutes a day to turn off your phone, shut out the world around you, and do nothing. Progress to two fifteen-minute intervals daily and then work up to one hour per week.
- **Medium:** Have a daily fifteen-minute do-nothing window in the morning and set aside two evenings a week or one weekend afternoon to do nothing.
- **Deep:** Start every day with a thirty-minute block of doing nothing and end every day with another thirty-minute block. Take a whole day once every two months to clear your schedule of activities and obligations and do nothing.

When You're Too Busy to Do Nothing

If you're wondering how you'll ever find the time to do nothing when getting through a single day requires juggling work, activities, family, and other responsibilities, don't worry. You will find the time because, in truth, even the busiest person has windows of time spent waiting or brief moments of procrastination that they can turn into do-nothing time. Some of this waiting or procrastination is hiding during work or in your usual Tuesday evening routine. Once you embrace doing nothing, those windows of waiting reshape themselves in your mind as available time. You can turn those short windows into luxurious moments when you embrace doing nothing.

You'll also find the time to do nothing because it is a very low-maintenance activity: you can do nothing anywhere, at any time. That's right; you don't need running shoes, an app, or a log-in to access the work network from outside the office. You don't need any special equipment for your do-nothing time. You also don't need to be anywhere specific for these activities. You can commit to doing nothing while sitting on a bus, waiting in line at the grocery store, or spending time in the lunchroom at work. Home or away, you'll easily be able to slip in your necessary restorative time to do nothing.

Even the busiest among us can find the time to practice a restorative do-nothing habit once a day. Start looking objectively at how you spend your hours. When you can see your day clearly, those windows of minutes spent waiting, your fringe hours, and your procrastination habits transform into available time for joyously doing nothing. Take that time back!

Use Time You Already Spend Waiting

There's no need to block off huge parts of your day to do nothing. Using small windows of waiting time is one of the easiest ways to incorporate doing nothing into your life. Making the time could be as simple as changing what you do and think about on your way to work. Normally you might be thinking about your job, your long commute, what's for dinner—all while half listening to the radio. Instead, turn the radio off and enjoy some rare but oh-so-necessary silence. Take note of your surroundings and let all those worries (the ones you really can't do anything about going five miles per hour on the freeway) disappear. Your time for doing nothing hasn't required a schedule overhaul but rather a small, easy tweak.

Likewise, rethink where your mind can be during the day if your body is committed to one spot. That ten-minute wait in line at the post office is usually spent letting out a few mental sighs about the person at the front of the line who can't decide between sending their parcel Ground or Priority Mail. Instead, take a few deep breaths, relax your shoulders, and enjoy ten minutes of letting your mind wander through things you're grateful for...like the delicious leftovers you'll have for lunch or the first signs of spring that have arrived.

Reclaim Your "Fringe Hours"

Another area where it's relatively easy to find time to do nothing: your "fringe hours"—right before you go to bed and right after you wake up. Most of us give up on getting anything done after eight o'clock. Too tired for the gym or getting housework done, we end up sitting on our couches watching Netflix. In the morning, we're rushing to get out the door because we stayed up late watching "just one more" episode, slept in, and now we're running late.

No more! Claim those fringe hours for joyously doing nothing. Finish the dishes, put the kids to bed, take the dog for a walk, and then...settle in to do nothing. The television is off, the phone is in Do Not Disturb mode, and you've got an hour or two of glorious time to yourself to unwind and let the day's stress slip away before bed.

In the morning, you're awake and refreshed—you went to bed on time!—*and* find yourself fifteen minutes ahead of schedule, so you spend it however you like. Fringe hours are a bounty of do-nothing time and the perfect place to start for those feeling overwhelmed by their daytime commitments.

Transform Your Procrastination Time

Another place to find do-nothing time: in your time-wasting and procrastination activities. C'mon, we all have them. It could be a sports team you follow a little too closely, refreshing ESPN.com multiple times a day for updates, or it could be a habit of checking multiple social media sites several times a day. Asking your manager about her ultramarathon hobby when you want to stretch a meeting out to make the workday a little shorter qualifies too. You can easily turn these little ten-minute time killers into do-nothing time.

Block Out the Noise Around You

Even if you live in a noisy and boisterous home, or your workplace is filled with chatter and overhead music, you can still find time for a do-nothing break to do nothing amid all that noise. If you learn to block out noise easily and overcome its distractions, you'll be able to find more moments in your days to do nothing. Here are some tips on learning to block out noise:

- Start with your eyes closed, take three or four deep breaths, and focus on thoughts of a calm and happy place, like your favorite place in nature, a cozy spot you read in, or your bed.
- After that, if you're ready, try to let your mind empty of any thoughts. Don't worry if you can't at first. Simply being calm and thinking good thoughts is restful, stress reducing, and restorative.
- If you notice a noise or pick up bits of conversation, just take note that you heard it and try to move your mind back to nothing or your favorite place.
- Think of that noise as ambient instead of specific. As in, it's not music or your coworker eating a sandwich noisily—it's just sound, like the hum of a generator or the vague rush of traffic outside.
- Don't fret if it takes a while to build up your skills for blocking out noise or if you find it easier some days than others. You're still getting that helpful and restful do-nothing time in, and that's what counts.

Schedule the Time

If you're struggling to commit to do-nothing time, schedule it on your calendar just like you would a work meeting or a dentist appointment. Set a reminder for five minutes before each scheduled time and make it a recurring event so it's built into your life. In an age of being able to do everything at any time, make a commitment to do nothing as frequently and for as long as you need.

Reclaim Time in Your Life: Say No

Half of the troubles of this life can be traced to saying yes too quickly and not saying no soon enough.

—Henry Wheeler Shaw, American Humorist

Many of us find ourselves overscheduled because we love to say yes. People hold onto a deeply held idea that you only say no if you absolutely have to—think "I'm sorry I can't help you move, but I have a funeral that afternoon"—and that saying yes is a good thing or the "right" thing to do.

Sure, saying yes is a good thing. It's a great thing. But saying yes shouldn't come at your own expense. *No* is a powerful and underused word. *No* doesn't mean you don't care; it means you care enough that you don't want to give someone less than your full attention, less than your best work, and less than your best effort. And you simply can't give everyone your best when you say yes to everything.

What if you said no more often?

- "No, I need a full eight hours of sleep to feel good, so I can't attend your late-evening event."
- "No, I think I'll be quite tired from an already full weekend, so I'll have to say no to that party on Sunday."
- "No, I can't give you 100 percent of my attention right now, so your request will have to wait."

Saying no isn't a rejection of someone or something—it's an honest and open response that saying yes wouldn't be best for you or for the other person. What if you felt no need to make up an excuse about why you can't come to a particular event? No fake "I wish I could but I have a conflict," but just a straight up truthful and bold "no, thanks" or "not tonight" or "I'm having a quiet night at home to myself." What if you not only said a polite "no thank you" but also had the audacity to tell the host, when they push further on why you can't make it, that you just want some time to yourself? What if you claimed your personal time the same way work claims your forty-plus hours a week?

Remember, you're your own CEO. You say how you spend your time. And if you want to spend it floating on a blow-up flamingo in the community pool rather than at the always-turns-ugly office trivia get-together, that's your right. Do not apologize because you would literally rather do nothing than go to a one-year-old's birthday party. Instead, claim your time as your own and do what *you* want to do with that time. Time that is completely unproductive and focused just on you is valuable and important!

Get comfortable with being a bit uncomfortable. Say no and don't qualify it with an excuse or a white lie about being busy. If pressed, tell the truth: I'm taking some quiet time to myself, not doing much of anything, because it feels great and it helps me enjoy life more. Boldly claim your time for doing nothing without apologies, excuses, or lies. Here are some ways to get used to saying no:

- **Light:** Designate one night a week for yourself and say no to any and all requests for your time on that night. Soon you'll have the confidence to reveal the real reasons behind your "no" RSVP.
- **Medium:** When asked why you can't volunteer/attend an event, tell the host you're taking some quiet time for yourself. Your candid confession may find a sympathizer who also craves time to do nothing!

- **Deep:** End a frequent and joyless commitment that you've been too scared to quit, such as a class, social group, or committee. You'll quickly find it was easier than you thought to extricate yourself. No one made you feel bad about it, and the time gained to do nothing will radically improve your mood and focus.

The Power of Connection

One of the reasons why it's tough to say no is because we can see, do, and connect in so many ways that we never could before. We can engage with our friends and family from anywhere through text messages, emails, direct messages, video chats, or phone calls. We can enjoy those people, let them know how much we care about them, make them laugh, and share with them at any time. It's truly remarkable! Your best friend can live a thousand miles away and still be a deep and present source of daily support in your life.

Using Connectivity Mindfully

All this engagement, all this connection, can sometimes take over your time and attention before you even realize it. You must actively manage your use of this wonderful technology or the white space in your life will quickly disappear. The fruits of technology—the ones that let your relationships flourish and make your life easier—can also leave you with no time for quiet introspection and replenishing silence. Doing nothing helps you get the best out of all this technology, but you do need to control how it impacts your life.

Doing nothing helps you reclaim what's great about all this choice and connection. You can block out all the wasteful chatter, ignore the advertisements for things you don't need or want, and identify the things you do need and want. You can make those small decisions quickly and without second-guessing yourself. Doing nothing is an essential component of actually enjoying this choice and possibility in our modern life.

The Challenge of Disconnecting to Do Nothing

It's so hard to turn your brain off these days and get some quiet. There are so many fun distractions. Television is so good right now and available on demand almost everywhere. There are so many ways to get messages from friends, relevant news about your city or town, updates about your favorite sports teams, juicy details on that celebrity split you are guiltily following, and those stunning photos of your friend's trip to India. It's all right there. And that makes it so hard to disconnect for your do-nothing time.

Remember, doing nothing is time for you to unwind and relax. And that will mostly mean being offline. If that scares you, fear not. Start small. You'll benefit from even the smallest change in your online habits. And when you start feeling these benefits—less stress, more focus— you'll put yourself in a feel-good feedback loop. The more time you spend offline doing nothing, the more you'll want to put your phone away and connect with yourself, friends, and the world around you.

Seven Ways to Start Disconnecting

1. Leave your phone at home for quick errands. Get used to that feeling of not having it in your pocket/bag.

2. Put your phone to sleep for the night. Leave it charging in another room—not your bedroom. Yes, dust off that alarm clock and start using it again.

3. Turn off push notifications for most of your apps.

4. Have a day offline. It could be once a week or once a month. It could be complete (you actually turn your phone off) or just partial (you only answer phone calls).

5. Set some evenings each week to be screen-free. This means no television, phone, iPad, or computer. Get used to, and start enjoying, the offline life.

6. Stop checking and returning messages immediately. Set a time each day for reading and replying to personal emails and messages.

7. Make a point of connecting with friends and family in person. You'll start to crave more real-life interaction and rely on your phone less to nurture and grow friendships.

Here's a guide to finding the level of connectivity that's right for you:

- **Light:** Turn that text conversation into a phone call. When you hit five minutes of messaging back-and-forth, suggest a real, live, old-school phone call instead.

- **Medium:** Put your phone away at mealtimes and when you're watching television. Get comfortable with single-tasking and enjoying those activities more.

- **Deep:** Take a break from one of your most-used social media accounts. Leave a "gone for a while" message up and ask people to call you or come by if they want to connect. Take the bold leap into mostly offline friendship and socializing.

Doing Nothing Is a Path to Greater Contentment

Better sleep, less anxiety, deeper relationships, less stress: there are so many reasons to make doing nothing a regular part of your life. The big one is that you will enjoy your life more. By regularly taking these restorative breaks, you prioritize your wellness (it feels good to do something positive for yourself), you make yourself a more engaged and present friend/sibling/parent/employee, and you get clarity on the things, people, and activities that make you feel good. As you read through all the ways to make doing nothing a part of your life, know that you are taking a simple and wonderful step forward that will reward you and the people around you.

Now let's look at the how and where of doing nothing with friends and family, at work, at home, and in other activities.

Family and Friends

Some people go to priests; others to poetry; I to my friends.
—Virginia Woolf, Writer

The joy of doing nothing is contagious. Once you're in the groove of taking these deeply relaxing breaks, your friends and family will start to notice a change in you. You'll have a new, calm energy. Joyfully doing nothing will make you a more present person with positive energy. Your friends and family will want to know where this change has come from, and you'll be eager to let them in on the secret. Your new level of relaxation and contentment could even help you bring others into the sweet fold of doing nothing. But how can you tell them about the joy doing nothing has brought you without the worry that they'll mistake this focused and restful relaxation technique for laziness? How can you explain that the time spent doing nothing is just as important to you as the time spent on other activities that contribute to wellness? How can you gently encourage them to do nothing with you?

In this chapter, we'll reflect on the many ways we interact—in person and online—and how to implement white spaces of time for doing nothing while simultaneously deepening your most cherished relationships. We'll explore how to introduce the concept to your inner circle and even show you how to do nothing together. And you'll discover ways to explain the philosophy of doing nothing in an easy and gentle manner so that you might coax your friends and family into adopting this joyfully rewarding habit.

> Your new level of relaxation and contentment
> could even help you bring others into the
> sweet fold of doing nothing.

Doing Nothing with a Family/Kids

If you're a parent, you might feel that you desperately need the calm, joyful reset of doing nothing. You're pulled in so many directions that these quick moments of relaxation might be exactly what you need to enjoy and power through your day. Trying to balance your own needs with those of your children and partner often leads to neglecting yourself. Your energy lags, and then you have even less motivation and time for self-care. Doing nothing can be an easy and simple way for parents to claim some personal time for themselves.

The beauty of doing nothing for parents is that it's so simple and so flexible that everyone can find the time and space to fit these breaks into their day. Yes, finding the time for self-care with children or babies at home can be challenging. If you're not fitting in your "would-be-nice to-dos" (like packing yourself a nutritious lunch) or even your "must-dos" (like eight hours of sleep), it can seem insurmountable to find the time to kick back and do nothing. But here's a secret: even the smallest amount of do-nothing time will pay you back exponentially. You'll gain a focus and efficiency from your do-nothing breaks that will help you get in those "must-dos" and also help you find the energy for those "would-be-nice to-dos." And unlike a lot of other types of self-care, doing nothing is incredibly easy to fit into any parent's schedule.

How Families Benefit from Doing Nothing

It's not just parents who need a deep and relaxing time-out: kids need it too! When everyone in the family gets the space and time to do nothing, the whole family wins. A new positive family rhythm is born from doing nothing. The reasons to get the whole family on board are manyfold: it's a frugal and easy self-care technique for parents and an entry point for the kind of deep, creative play that some children unfortunately miss out on in today's digital age.

You'll Teach Your Kids the Art of Stillness

If you're thinking that telling your kids to just "do nothing" might initially be...challenging, you're certainly not alone. Most kids are used to being busy, so when they aren't being taught, coached, or entertained by a screen, they may find themselves bored. And their boredom probably won't lead them to immediately enjoy stillness; they'll most likely ask you for more distractions and entertainment. Nonetheless, teaching your kids to do nothing, to deeply relax and calm their minds, will make them less stressed and more in tune with themselves. And it's probably not going to be as difficult to teach as you fear.

Teaching Kids to Do Nothing

Doing nothing for kids should be the same as it is for adults: simple, fun, and easy. So start your children out with age-appropriate and kid-specific short breaks to relax. Make your initial attempts very brief: ask them to do just three minutes of a calm and restful activity like sitting and imagining themselves at their favorite park or beach or watching clouds outside. Ask them to sit quietly and think of just one thing, like a relaxing and positive experience or hobby. The older the child, the longer these sessions of doing nothing can be.

Once your kids are comfortable with these short breaks, encourage them to give their brains a break. The concept of thinking of nothing and letting go of worries will be appropriate for older children. Ask them to try to think of nothing and treat it like a game. Ask them to note if a thought pops into their head and what it is. For younger children, keep the do-nothing break centered around a light thinking activity with a fun objective, like remembering a trip or imagining themselves somewhere that's special to them. This kind of easy do-nothing activity, even if done for just a few minutes a day, will give your kids that same restorative break that adults need. You'll find that your kids will be able to focus better and even use do-nothing techniques to calm themselves down.

As with other skills you teach your kids, modeling the behavior yourself is one of the fastest and most effective ways to show them what to do. Let your children see that you are not puttering around the house picking up socks or spending time on your phone. You're doing nothing. And that's okay. It's okay to let your mind and body be quiet. Show them that you are comfortable with doing nothing and that it makes you feel good. Verbalize that taking a real break—no screens, no checking things off a list—helps you enjoy your life more.

Be the example and leader in your household of doing nothing and your children will follow. Children learn by example, and if their example is a parent that prioritizes self-care and engages with the people around them, they will imitate those behaviors. When you tell them to sit in the backyard and enjoy the sun, they will do just that because they saw you doing the same yesterday—no distractions, just enjoying nature, resting, and doing nothing. As you lead by example, the children will open up to restful, undistracted breaks.

Here are three different ways to approach teaching children to do nothing:

- **Light:** Sit with your four-year-old and help him quietly think about one of his favorite places or experiences, like the community pool or playing at his best friend's house. Set a timer for three minutes and ask him to see if he can be quiet and just think of his special activity for that long.
- **Medium:** Ask your seven-year-old to take a do-nothing break before she starts her school assignments each night. Encourage her to spend five minutes trying to not think of anything.
- **Deep:** As a family, build an evening bedtime ritual around doing nothing. Have your children practice doing nothing for a set amount of time, building up to ten minutes, after they have brushed their teeth and are in their pajamas.

Add Downtime to a Child's Busy Day

Doing nothing is a great activity to add to your child's schedule. Children have so many excellent after-school and extracurricular options these days—dramatic arts, sports, music, robotics/STEM clubs, and service organizations—and your kids probably want to try them all! Today's kids are lucky enough to fill most of their waking hours with fun opportunities to create, play, and compete; but as you look at their schedules, ask yourself if they also have slots of time to do nothing. As they learn to appreciate stillness, it's important to be sure they have time to practice it regularly. If you make it an expected part of their day, it's easier to make it a priority—to say no to a playdate or a birthday party because it conflicts with that downtime.

Here are three levels of do-nothing downtime that you can incorporate into a busy kid's schedule:

- **Light:** Reserve a few hours each weekend for your child to unwind and do nothing. If you don't have any hours available, you'll know you've overcommitted to activities and events and it's time to cancel some plans.
- **Medium:** Make a regular practice of doing nothing three times a week for fifteen minutes. Schedule this in as you would band practice. Aim to have everyone in the family take this break at the same time.
- **Deep:** Have everyone in the family practice doing nothing for thirty minutes a day. Ideally you make this time first thing in the morning or as part of your evening sleep routine.

Doing Nothing Can Lead to Quality Playtime

Once your children have become comfortable with deeply relaxing and doing nothing distraction-free, they'll glean all the same benefits from it that you do. Their creativity will be sparked, and they will move on from their breaks to deep creative, mental, or physical play. This brain reboot will remove their distractions and allow them to engage in the kind of play and activity that feeds their brain and body. For younger children, doing nothing will lead them to the kind of open-ended, limited-toy, imagination- and nature-focused play that they need for proper development. For teenagers, doing nothing can be the perfect lead-in to studying and homework or even to sports or music practice.

In pediatric occupational therapist Angela J. Hanscom's book *Balanced and Barefoot: How Unrestricted Outdoor Play Makes for Strong, Confident, and Capable Children,* she recommends three hours a day of outdoor play for children for optimal development. Hanscom notes that today's modern children spend so much time indoors participating in structured activities and screen time that they don't at first know how to play outdoors. Children need time to warm up to open-ended creative and physical play, particularly if they aren't doing this kind of play regularly. If you want your children to spend more time outdoors or in open-ended play, a brief session of doing nothing could be their entry point. Use that distraction-free time, even a brief five minutes, to help your children reset.

Here are three ideas of varying intensity that can help deepen playtime quality for kids:

- **Light:** Play in the backyard with just nature and a ball. Stow the water table and ride-on toys in the garage and let your children engage and explore outside without distraction.
- **Medium:** Make a large freestyle drawing. Roll out a length of butcher paper on the floor or across a table, put out some crayons or

colored pencils, and let your children create without any demands, objectives, or complicated crafts. (Leave the sparkles, stickers, and such for another day.)

- **Deep:** Start a practice of keeping a daily journal. For younger children it can be a journal of drawings they make about their day, and older children can write an age-appropriate amount about what they did that day and how they feel about it.

Budget-Friendly Parental Self-Care

Doing nothing is a wonderful form of self-care for parents because it's free and doesn't require hiring a babysitter. Many parents don't have the financial resources to take a weekly date night: dinner and a movie, with the hourly rate for the neighborhood babysitter added in, quickly increases the cost of an evening out. A weekly massage or a night out for beers for one of you requires financial investment, planning, and asking your partner to solo parent for the evening. When you make time to do nothing, you get quality self-care time in without inconveniencing your partner or calling around for a babysitter.

Not only is doing nothing a free form of self-care, but it can also actually help you save money by curbing your casual spending. For example:

- You're less likely to order takeout due to sheer exhaustion when you take moments to refresh yourself and do nothing.
- When you intentionally do nothing, you don't need to buy things as a quick pick-me-up. No need to spend money on a "treat" or buy

something out of stress when you've already given yourself the free gift of doing nothing.

Doing nothing becomes a go-to way to de-stress and, wonderfully, there's zero impact to the family budget from simply relaxing and doing nothing.

Doing Nothing Helps Caregivers

If you have obligations to take care of aging parents, whether they live with you or you take care of them outside of work hours, you may also wonder where you will find the time to do nothing. The demands of family often supersede finding any time for self-care. When the work is urgent and necessary—such as cooking meals or doing household tasks your parents can no longer do for themselves—it seems selfish not to help them have a good quality of life in any way you can. You want to be there for them, taking them to doctor's appointments and social engagements they can no longer get to on their own. But it's easy to end up with no time for yourself. Where will you find the time to do nothing when there's hardly time for you to do something?

Start with those fringe hours (right before bed and early in the morning). Even if it's a short window of time, you will see benefits. If you have parents living with you or are on call for them, be flexible. Aim to get that do-nothing time in every day, with the understanding that it just won't happen some days. Remind yourself that some time is better than no time. Find ways to do nothing when you're with your parents. If your parents need a lot of rest time, use that time to do nothing—even if it's just sitting in their garden while they watch television inside. If your parents are mostly housebound, make a quiet spot for yourself that you can use to relax and do nothing. If you drive your parents to appointments or to get groceries, use that time spent waiting for them to get your do-nothing practice in.

The restorative and stress-reducing power of doing nothing is ideal for caregivers. Taking care of aging or ill parents is a taxing job physically and emotionally. Doing nothing is flexible; it can be done anywhere, and it works for stress reduction—even in small doses. If you are putting hours and days into caring for others, make it a priority to also take care of yourself with a few sessions a week of doing nothing.

How to Find the Time to Do Nothing in a Busy Family

If you haven't gone to the bathroom with the door closed in five years or your Google calendar is jammed with complicated carpools for three different soccer schedules, this section is for you. Because you definitely deserve this do-nothing time in your life. No matter how your schedule looks, you'll find pockets of time hidden in there. The beauty of doing nothing is that it can be done anywhere at any time.

Use Those "Fringe Hours"

The primary place to start finding your do-nothing time is in those fringe hours we discussed in the first chapter. The fringe hours, the ones that we are usually too tired to take advantage of, really can become a wealth of usable time with just a few simple lifestyle changes. Scavenge that time for a short window to yourself. It could be:

- Waking up before those early riser children to enjoy a little morning peace and quiet.
- Doing one small piece of prep work—putting the kids' clothing out, packing daycare bags—the night before so that you can squeeze in a bit of time when the kids are eating breakfast.
- Reclaiming part of your night. If mornings are unavoidably packed, look to the evening. Everyone can find twenty minutes before they go to bed for themselves. Set an alarm on your phone for thirty minutes before you want to go to bed and put down or shut off whatever you are doing when it goes off.

Let Some Housework Wait

Set a mantra that the laundry can wait. Parents often use downtime at home, the hours that children are napping or nicely occupied with Lego construction, to work. They open their work computer or knock out some household chores while their children enjoy their own do-nothing activities. As the children happily engage in a singular and refreshing activity, parents rush around trying to "catch up" and then hit the evening hours exhausted and ready to sit comatose on the couch once the last bedtime story has been read.

Rethink what is most important for the family. The laundry will get done; it always does. There will be a meal for dinner; there always is. But will there be an engaged and refreshed parent there to help the three-year-old dress himself? Will there be a focused parent at the dinner table ready to listen and respond because they took a moment for themselves in the afternoon? Make some of that "catch up" time be for you. Even a short five minutes of deep breaths and a blank mind will pay you back with some Zen and happiness that will benefit you and your family.

Take Advantage of Your Location

If you work outside the home, use your office as your do-nothing venue. Block off your lunch hour twice a week for do-nothing time. No calling for appointments for your kids or having a conference call with your spouse about managing household tasks. Set that time aside for yourself and for doing nothing. A bonus about doing nothing while at work: there aren't any kids to disrupt you or nagging household tasks to distract you. For parents, particularly parents of young children, your workplace can be an ideal location to get some do-nothing time in. You may even take twenty minutes to yourself in the office after the workday is over, unwinding and releasing the stress of the day before you head out to pick up or meet the kids at home for dinner.

> For parents, particularly parents of young children, your workplace can be an ideal location to get some do-nothing time in.

If you're a stay-at-home parent, use those quiet moments—even the really brief ones!—to find time for yourself. When you get windows of time to yourself, kick things off with fifteen minutes of doing nothing no matter where you are: in the car, sitting in a coffee shop, at home alone. For example, if you arrive home with two kids asleep in their car seats, enjoy it. Sit in the car, relax, and let your mind go blank. Don't think about all the stuff you could be doing inside, everything that's waiting to get done. Turn your phone off and just enjoy the quiet of two little people snoring and no one demanding anything of you.

Do Nothing Mentally, If Not Physically

If you can't physically be alone, aim to escape mentally. If your seven-year-old needs you to lay on the floor next to his bed and hold his hand while he falls asleep, use that time. Likewise, your mind can be anywhere even if you're trapped under a sleeping newborn and can't leave the couch. Resist those pesky screens, leave the phone and remote out of reach, let go of any worries, feel your mind empty, and just let yourself be.

This also applies to being physically idle. While it's not ideal to do any type of work while doing nothing, it may at times be the only way to fit it into your day. So, if you're the parent doing evening cleanup, try to use that time wiping the dinner table down and loading the dishwasher to take a mental escape. We'll talk more about doing nothing while performing light tasks in the Home chapter, but remember, while picking up scattered toys may have your body, it doesn't have your mind. Use those windows of light, easy activity or instances when the children are occupied to give your brain a break with doing nothing.

Work with Your Family's Schedule

Do not fret if your do-nothing time is just a few times a week and consists of a slow walk with an idle brain while your oldest is at hockey practice. For some parents, their time to do nothing may be just a few minutes here and there as they make the most of waiting in line, going through the car wash, or even going to the bathroom. Frequent short breaks to do nothing work best for the unpredictable or demanding family schedule, and they can still be very beneficial.

Change is inevitable. As your family grows and its schedule or demands follow suit, take note of new ways and pockets of time to do nothing. For example:

- A child may give up napping but can now keep himself occupied with an activity for longer durations, giving you time to do nothing.
- You may be in a season of more driving, so use that time before picking up or after dropping off children to turn the radio off and let go of your worries. Be a relaxed and fully focused driver and savor having no distractions.

For the time-strapped, even the act of giving yourself this time, of being intentional about doing something just for you, has a positive effect. It feels great to be present and relaxed and without worry. You give a lot of yourself to the people around you, and this moment to do nothing is a gift you give yourself.

Create a New Family Ritual

Make doing nothing a family ritual. It could be an opportunity to come together during busy evenings or to gather before breakfast or to segue from a busy weekend morning into a quiet weekend afternoon. Open your minds and your schedule to doing nothing together. Just as you have certain activities or phrases or special meals that are part of your family culture, you can also have this activity that you use to reset and relax. Incorporate doing nothing into your family lore. You may have a tradition of a brief ritual before dinner, either a prayer or saying things you're thankful for. These rituals ground your children and promote positive thoughts. If you already have these traditions and rituals, you'll find it easy to add a break for doing nothing. When you gather as a family, simply ask everyone to take a few minutes to clear their minds and relax before you begin your activity or meal.

A more relaxed and engaged family rhythm appears when you do nothing together. Less rushing, more thought. Less whining, more relaxed and engaged activity. The benefits to families are manyfold when you join together in easy and relaxed time for doing nothing. Start with a small change in one of your weekly routines. Perhaps Friday night is changed from movie night to do-nothing night every other week. Or implement a weekend afternoon rule of no screens and no playing with traditional toys. The beauty of doing nothing as a family is that everyone—parents included—will get that time free of screens and obligations and stress. Together you'll create a new peaceful and joyful rhythm by taking restorative breaks to do nothing alone and together.

Here are three ideas for family rituals that support doing nothing:

- **Light:** Switch up those Saturday morning cartoons for some do-nothing time and relaxed play for adults and kids.
- **Medium:** Commit to outdoor time as a family once a day, rain or shine. Take this break together before or after dinner each evening. A short walk in the neighborhood or simply a jaunt through the backyard to pick up leaves will refresh all of you and get you into the do-nothing mind-set.

- **Deep:** Take a break from your toys and screens. Box up some of your toys with lights and sounds, leaving the most simple and open-ended play ones out, and take the iPads and laptops away for a week. Use this toy and screen break to create a calmer household with do-nothing breaks and lots of deep imaginative play for your kids.

Share the Concept with Extended Family

When and if you feel comfortable, you could also bring the do-nothing movement to your holiday celebrations with extended family. Ask family if you can all have a "quiet year"—half as many dishes made, half as many planned family outings, half the presents, half the time. Turn your all-day Thanksgiving into a peaceful late-afternoon shindig with just your favorite dishes. Boldly reclaim the true meaning behind these holidays: rest and connection with the ones you love.

Here are three ideas to bring the joy of doing nothing to your family's holiday event:

- **Light:** Suggest trimming the heavy and elaborate menu items so that no one is stuck in the kitchen cooking and cleaning up for most of the day. Instead, everyone makes one favorite that they cook ahead of time. Fewer dishes and stress and more time together will get your family into the do-nothing spirit.
- **Medium:** Cut your holiday events and obligations in half. When family ask why you're not attending, explain that you want to really enjoy the holiday and not be so stressed out this year. Aim to really engage with your family at the events you do attend.

- **Deep:** Have your first no-gift Christmas. Skip the stress and expense of traditional gift giving and instead give each other the beautiful gift of your time and attention. Have a fun and easy and gift-free gathering. Use those saved funds to donate to a favorite cause or splurge on a restaurant or catered meal together.

Build Deeper Friendships by Doing Nothing Together

Family, friendships, and community are vital parts of a life well lived. Everyone needs people who know and love us, and we need to know and love people like we need air and water. After all, being lonely has far-reaching negative impacts on physical and mental health and quality of life. Friends make life more fun. Friends give you honest feedback about yourself that helps you know yourself better. When your friends lean on you for support, help, or advice, it contributes to your feeling of having a purpose. And having a purpose contributes to your overall happiness. Clearly, friendship is an integral part of having a content and purposeful life. But while we know friendship is important, it's not always so easy to know how to maintain or even deepen existing friendships.

Building friendships as an adult sometimes feels like a mystery. How do you turn an outer circle friend, the one you see every six weeks, into an inner circle friend, the one that you can call in a crisis and who would do the same in turn? How did pencil sharing turn into being her maid of honor? How did the blind luck of buying your specific house give you the gift of a deep, decades-long friendship with your neighbors? Guess what's at the root of many of those relationships? Doing nothing together.

Yes, doing nothing together is actually a step forward in a relationship. The bonds of friendship really can be strengthened when you spend time together doing nothing. When you spend time together in unproductive and joyful ways, you get the opportunity to open up to each other in unstructured ways, learn more about each other through meandering conversations, and thereby deepen the friendship. This time together also becomes a memorable shared experience, and shared experiences are the foundation of long friendships. When you spend time together, you are more likely to accept your friends for who they are, without judgment. We all want to be seen and understood by our friends, and we crave acceptance of our best traits and little-known quirks. These details of friendships create a strong bedrock for lasting relationships.

The following are several benefits of doing nothing with a friend.

Learn New Things about Each Other

Have you ever found out something about a friend that completely changed your perception of them? Perhaps she shared a story from her childhood that helped you understand her view of the world in a new way. Or you found out about a small quirk of his, something he kept hidden for fear of judgment or because it didn't line up with his public persona. Or maybe it was something small, a throwaway little bit of themselves—which section of the newspaper they start reading first or how they hate having their birthday celebrated—that lines up precisely with yourself, and your connection to this friend and the feeling of not being alone in this world both blossom.

These are the ways friends make deeper connections in their do-nothing time together. You've created a space for these stories to come out, the ones you thought were insignificant or that you never found the right time or space to share. It's hard to have these connections when you're working intensely side by side or are at a crowded and loud dinner party or when your time together is busy watching kids. But if you can find purposefully quiet and slow time to spend together, these beautiful stories and connections will come out and grow.

Move an Outer Circle Friend Into the Inner Circle

Can you pinpoint when your good friend moved from just a friend to your inner circle? If you're used to doing "things" with your friends, such as meeting for spin class every Wednesday or seeing each other when you volunteer as tutors, you might not have the space or time to take your friendship to the next level. But hanging out with nothing on the agenda and an open spirit and mind? That leads to fun and open-ended opportunities to widen your circle of friends.

Show Your Friends You Love Them Just the Way They Are

Another way we deepen friendship: accepting each other for who we are, without judgment. When you do nothing together, you invite closeness that can lead to shared "confessions" that take a friendship to the next level. Maybe your friend tells you that he's taking swimming lessons because he never learned as a kid. Maybe you share that you're secretly loving the new teen book series. (Maybe you even share that you're incorporating doing nothing into your life!)

When you accept a friend's secrets and/or share something private about yourself, you show your friends that those quirks are nothing to be ashamed of, but rather an accepted and celebrated part of who they are.

How to Share the Joy of Doing Nothing with Friends

One of the best ways to make a positive action (like doing nothing) into a habit is to surround yourself with people who also have the same positive habit. So, sharing the joy of doing nothing—encouraging and supporting your friends as they, too, make the time to regularly relax by doing nothing—will not only help them, but it will also help you too.

Introduce Doing Nothing to Your Friends Gradually

Start small when introducing your friends to the concept of doing nothing. Perhaps you answer the "Why are you so Zen?" question from a friend who has noticed your relaxed and blissed-out state with, "Oh, I'm making more time for myself." Be a little vague. When you get a chance, suggest a small change in plans that gives everyone an opportunity to sleep in or do a bit less. Bring a few of your high-preparation and intense gatherings down into a gentler state that gives everyone a real break. Take the pressure off by suggesting simple meals, fresh air, and a focus on quality time together rather than detailed itineraries.

Once your friends have spent some low-key time with you, tell them you've been practicing doing nothing, taking deep and restful breaks regularly. Tell them how these breaks have helped you—be it better sleep, more energy, or feeling more present and engaged when you're with them. If they're open to the idea, suggest some do-nothing time as part of your time together. It could be a short reset before you head out for a vigorous activity or a wind-down exercise after a busy evening. Commit to putting your phones away for ten minutes and deeply relaxing together. Like discovering a new hiking trail, restaurant, or book together, doing nothing can be a fun bonding experience for any relationship.

Explaining Your Do-Nothing Habit to Friends and Family

There is no need to keep your do-nothing activities secretive and solo. Ask your friends along, reveal your newfound focus on doing nothing, and use these activities to deepen your friendships and accept each other just as you are.

- **Light:** Reveal one of your do-nothing activities to a friend.
- **Medium:** Ask a friend to join you for something different from your usual crazy morning spent coaching youth soccer—a morning spent on a park bench, coffee and donuts in hand, watching squirrels run up trees.
- **Deep:** Ask your friend(s) to share one of their favorite do-nothing activities with you. Tell them you want to be a better friend and that being let in on—even joining in on—their casual and usually solo ways to unwind would be a great gift to your friendship.

Slow Down and Do Nothing Together

Once you've convinced those around you how great doing nothing is, you can start to do nothing with friends and family. What makes a good do-nothing activity to do with friends? It should meet the same criteria as your own do-nothing activities—unproductive, simple, and fun—but there should be some room to take different paths and end the activity at different times.

- If you're used to intense evenings playing Settlers of Catan, suggest a leftovers potluck (only bring leftovers from your fridge or food basics like bananas—no freshly made three-grain salads) and a very slow game of Snakes and Ladders.
- Ask friends to come and hang out with you in a park with no agenda or accoutrements. Lay in the grass, chat, and let the day take you where it may. It could be as simple as feeling the sun on your face, your shoes and socks off, the sweet smell of fresh-cut grass and the sounds of a string quartet busking nearby.
- You might even find yourself with time to make *new* friends when you slow down. Doing nothing will help you relax and make you a more per-sonable, genuine, and happier reflection of yourself. Doing nothing also might make you available—it's easier for you to say yes to new things and to seek out opportunities for friendship if you're not exhausted from a packed but unfulfilling schedule. This new view has you chatting with a stranger at the laundromat on a Thursday night and asking her if she wants to grab a beer next door once the dryer cycle finishes.

Enjoy those moments together with no urgency to put a label on your activity or make it meaningful or productive.

As we connect over these simple and unproductive activities, as we rebrand "time wasters" as soul- and brain-nourishing exercises, we make the movement of doing nothing a more accepted and celebrated act of self-care. Here are some more ideas for doing nothing with friends:

- **Light:** Skip the usual elaborate Sunday brunch at the place with the long line and grab takeout from a local café. Take your food back to someone's house for a viewing of a movie and naps on the couch.
- **Medium:** Invite your busy friends over for an unplanned and unscripted evening. Order pizza and set up a bubble-blowing machine as entertainment.
- **Deep:** Cancel your onerous book club, the one where all the members are too busy to read the book anyway. Instead, start a do-nothing club. The menu will be whatever you can find in your refrigerator and people are welcome to eat the remains of the lunch they packed for work. The activity, discussion, and menu won't be planned but will occur organically. It will be a chance to deeply relax together with no big agenda, onerous hosting, or detailed plans to bog things down.

...

Doing nothing with family and friends is not only a way to lower your own stress and gain more energy—it's a way to deepen your relationships. Everyone can use a break: your parents, your kids, and your friend that's always on the go. You can be the one to bring that break to them. You can be the friend or sister or parent that not only gives permission to do nothing but also shows everyone how to do it. And when you make this relaxed, restorative, and simple activity a part of those relationships, you make more room for knowing and supporting each other. Remember to start small: ask your preschooler to sit still and be quiet with you for a few minutes or suggest a more relaxed and intimate gathering for your next meet-up with friends. Share your joy in doing nothing by not only sharing how to do it but also by sharing all that you gain from it. Share your increased energy by helping a friend in need. Share your new focus by listening to someone without distraction. Share that the hosts need not put on an elaborate spread and slave away in the kitchen; a simple meal will do because you're there to see and be with them. The joy of doing nothing lets us see so clearly what's important to us, and family and friends are at the top of the list.

Work

Don't confuse having a career with having a life.
—Hillary Clinton, US Politician

Just as you deserve breaks in your non-work hours, you have earned moments in your workday to disconnect, relax, and recharge your batteries. The good news: doing nothing will actually help your performance at work. Taking regular breaks to relax and empty your mind will help you return to work refreshed and focused. You get new, creative ideas when you clear your head. You are more productive overall. And you feel better about yourself and enjoy your life more when you do your best at your job.

Pride in your work and feeling needed and useful contribute to contentment and daily happiness. Most of us spend a good portion of our week, and our life, at work. It's important to have a positive work life, as it takes up so much of your time and energy. Plus, unless you're independently wealthy or someone else is footing all your bills, work is a necessity. So why not use the power of doing nothing to help you enjoy work more *and* help you do your best?

What Is Doing Nothing at Work?

You may be wondering how you can apply some joyful do-nothing time to your job...while still remaining employed. Doing nothing at work isn't about slacking off or foisting work onto others. Doing nothing at work allows you to:

- Set boundaries
- Give yourself clear breaks
- Have clarity about what work is necessary and urgent
- Give yourself a chance to do your best
- Find balance
- Rethink your job if you're disenchanted

This will *not* be a primer on how to discreetly take a twenty-minute nap in the janitorial closet, how to pass off work onto gullible coworkers, or how to do the bare minimum to stay employed.

What Does Doing Nothing at Work Look Like?

Fifteen minutes with your eyes closed in the middle of your workday is rejuvenating, joyful, and intentional. That time to yourself, with no distractions, an open mind, and a relaxed body, is a well-deserved part of your day.

Understanding how to do nothing at work is easy when you compare it to procrastination. Both are breaks from work—but the end results show you what a big difference there is between the two. Doing nothing leads to more productivity, more happiness, and more energy.

Doing nothing...	Procrastination...
Is fulfilling and satiating.	Leaves you feeling empty and unsatisfied.
Allows you return to the tasks and work at hand with renewed vigor and a clear mind.	Leads you to reluctantly return to work with a feeling of dread.
Leads to a more enjoyable workday and better performance at work.	Leads to more procrastination.
Is purposeful and performance enhancing.	Is wracked with guilt and secrecy, which steals what little enjoyment you get from it.
Need not be secretive.	Is often done surreptitiously.

You also can't embrace your procrastination activities as you would a do-nothing activity because, well, you're trying to hide the fact that you're not working from your coworkers and the boss. You're surreptitiously scrolling through your phone that you're hiding under your desk, panicked someone is going to see you. Or you're spending a few too many minutes in the lunch room flipping through a newspaper, knowing that a supervisor could be looking at the clock and noting that you're not back on shift yet. On the other hand, doing nothing is taking the time to restart your brain and take a brief but deeply restful break.

Want to implement doing nothing into your work life right away? Here are three levels of doing nothing at work:

- **Light:** Simply take your morning coffee break silently and without any distractions. Learn to savor and enjoy the restorative power of doing nothing once every day.

- **Medium:** Use doing nothing to leave work at work. End your work-day with a break to do nothing and let any thoughts of your job go before you head home.
- **Deep:** Work less. Turn down overtime shifts, set boundaries for your workload and say no to going after that promotion. Let doing nothing center you on your values and what brings you the most fulfillment.

How Should You Share Your Habit with Your Employer?

To make doing nothing part of your workday and not have it appear that you are underperforming, first assess the culture of your workplace. If it's a workplace that values personal development and stress reduction techniques, simply say to anyone who asks that you are taking a short break to meditate. If it's a coworker, he or she probably won't have any further questions, but if it's your boss or manager, you should offer a more thorough explanation. Tell them...

- You're practicing taking more mindful breaks with no distractions to have better focus at work.
- It helps your productivity.

Most employers love hearing that you're taking care of yourself so you can be a better employee. You can even share your break plan and goals with your boss and clarify that you want to have more focus and energy for work after these breaks. If you have an open and forward-thinking employer, they may even want to incorporate some of the do-nothing philosophy into the workplace.

The following are some ideas for bringing the do-nothing culture to your workplace:

- **Suggest a quiet room for breaks.** This request could go to your human resources department or a workplace wellness committee. Ask for a space that is designated for employees to enjoy silence— no eating or talking or cell phones—during the workday.
- **Get a reminder.** Ask that break reminder software be installed on computers to remind workers to take breaks from staring at their screens to prevent eyestrain, stretch their legs and shoulders to prevent injury, and move around to help their productivity.
- **Be sure you're informed.** If it's not readily available, known, or implemented, ask for the employee break rules and schedule to be posted. This is especially important if the workplace culture pressures employees to not take breaks. Breaks are important and necessary not only for productivity and performance but for health and wellness.

If you need to explain your do-nothing breaks to a boss or manager, present them as a productivity tool—something to help you do more for the company. Explain to your boss that several silent breaks during the day, mere minutes to clear your mind and reset, help you engage with your work and give you more energy. If they are uncomfortable with this idea, simply ask for a trial basis of taking breaks. You can wow them with your increased productivity in a few weeks to get them on board with the do-nothing philosophy.

Getting Caught Doing Nothing

If you haven't shared your plan with your employer and you are "caught" doing nothing, be honest. Say that you are taking a short break to clear your mind. Be truthful and to the point. Remember what doing nothing looks like. Staring off into the distance looks quite different than, say, being caught in an empty office on a personal phone call or slipping back to your desk after taking an extended lunch. This time you make for yourself to do nothing should be restorative and uninterrupted by screens or other procrastination activities. Your boss or coworker might be surprised to catch you in quiet reverie, but it won't reflect badly on your character or your work.

If your workplace prefers that personal development and stress reduction happen outside of work hours, simply say you are taking a short break or "Oops, caught me daydreaming." Then adjust your time for doing nothing or your method. Remember, you can do nothing pretty much anywhere at any time, so if you need to squeeze it in standing at a photocopier, you can. If taking twenty minutes to do nothing is too obvious in your workplace, then take several shorter breaks and use any thoughtless or easy tasks as a time to joyfully do nothing.

How Doing Nothing Can Improve Your Performance at Work

It may seem counterintuitive, but doing nothing helps you do your best at work. You're able to see what the important work is and get it done when you've cleared your mind and rested. This restorative break helps you resist procrastination activities like goofing off on your phone, increasing your capacity for work.

> Taking breaks to do nothing allows you to give your full attention and energy to your work.

Doing nothing allows you to focus on work without the near-constant impulse to distract yourself. Fewer distractions—I'm looking at you, Twitter—lets you engage deeply with your work. When you really dive into the meat of your responsibilities, when it feels easy to work hard, you really start to enjoy your job more. These pauses can provide clarity on what you love about your job (and the motivation to find more of that work!). These pauses can give you more fire to be great at what you do. In this way, doing nothing can be a stepping stone to career success.

Boost Your Energy

Taking breaks to do nothing during your workday (and in your personal life) can give you the same restorative power that a week off work does. The vim that returned to your work after that tropical vacation—you can get that kind of benefit by incorporating joyfully doing nothing into your life. And you don't have to pay for airfare and a hotel to do it.

Giving yourself a brain break with doing nothing is like rebooting a frozen computer. We power down, reset, and start back up fresh and ready to go. This shows in your focus for work and your enjoyment of it. It's easier to get that to-do list checked off, to come up with new ideas, to power through the tough and demanding work after you have rebooted your brain with doing nothing. In a 2011 University of Illinois psychology study, two groups were asked to memorize numbers with one group getting breaks and the other group working continuously. The group that took two short breaks from the main task during a fifty-minute work session showed better results and focus than the group that took no breaks. We can flourish at work with short breaks to do nothing. So, empty all that cached data and trash, close out and restart all those programs running in your head, and reap the benefit of a mental restart with doing nothing. You'll return to your work with greater efficiency, ready to perform.

Physically Reset Your Body

Changing your posture while you do nothing also improves your work performance. Get up from being hunched over your desk for hours and take a brisk walk while clearing your mind, or simply move from a standing position to a seated one to spark a new energy and focus when you return to work. If possible, use physical movement to differentiate your do-nothing time from your work time. Whatever position your work keeps you in—standing, sitting, walking—do the opposite when you take time to do nothing. This physical change will give you a boost of energy when you return to work. Researchers from Baylor University found that employees who took physical breaks earlier—before a number of hours of work had elapsed—had fewer complaints of eyestrain, headaches, and lower back pain than employees who waited longer to take a break. Employees who took morning breaks also reported having more energy, better concentration, and more motivation to return to work.

Want to make a physical break a part of your workday? Here are three ways to implement a do-nothing physical break:

- **Light:** Stretch! Do a few simple neck, back, and hip flexor stretches on your first break of the day to get your body out of "work posture" and to get the blood flowing.
- **Medium:** Take the stairs during a morning break. Leave your phone at your desk and walk up, and then down, one or two flights of stairs.
- **Deep:** Use an early break for daily push-ups. Add one push-up each day until you reach your goal, be it ten or one hundred.

Even Out Your Bursts of Productivity

Giving yourself a planned break to do nothing can also help you work at a more consistent speed throughout the day. For many people, the workday just drags on with only lunchtime to break up the day, and it's very challenging to do focused and quality work in four-hour stints. A report from DeskTime, an app that tracks employee's computer time, found that the highest-performing employees tended to work for fifty-two minutes followed by a seventeen-minute break. Obviously, taking frequent breaks makes for consistent productivity.

Instead of slogging through hours of work, use "doing nothing" to break up the work and even out your productivity. If your work culture simply doesn't allow for a break every hour, power through two hours first thing in the morning with the promise of fifteen minutes just to yourself at the end of that period to do nothing with. The next segment of two hours has your lunch break at the end of it, and after that you can cruise through the afternoon, get another do-nothing break in the midafternoon—as your colleagues are throwing back a late-day coffee or wasting their time on social media to get through the afternoon slump—and then finish the day with the promise of quitting time. If you reserve these two short breaks for doing nothing, you can push yourself in volume and quality right up to the break time. Breaks to do nothing keep you motivated all day by giving you that "back from vacation" energy and focus.

Goof Off on Your Phone Less

The sweet distraction of Twitter and many other social media apps and news websites are so tempting when you feel tired and burnt out. Feeling you've arrived at a dead end with what you're working on? Open your Instagram feed to avoid thinking about it. Dreading a certain task that's landed in your inbox? Start a message thread with a bunch of friends and turn that thirty-minute task into two hours of painful and halting work. In a 2016 CareerBuilder survey of employers and employees, two out of three employees that had a smartphone at work said they checked it at least several times a day while working. Eighty-two percent of employees with smartphones kept them within their sight at work. A cure for chronic smartphone procrastination at work: breaks to do nothing.

The problem with constant social media checks is that they're often done without really asking yourself why you're doing them, and you probably don't feel refreshed or motivated after you do them. The way doing nothing makes you feel—refreshed and present—makes scrolling through the same four apps on your phone six times a day like a zombie unappealing. Doing nothing is intentional—you shut out the world and take calm, undistracted time for yourself. When you feel an impulse to check your personal email or a news website, take a short break to do nothing instead. Taking one or two breaks to do nothing during the day will help you stay present and engaged with your work and kick the habit of goofing off on your phone.

Cutting these online distractions from your workday will make you a more engaged and valuable employee.

When we make it a priority to do nothing, even for short bursts of time, we relearn how to shut out all the noise—online and offline—around us. The skill it takes to do nothing is the same skill you need to cut out the time you waste online at work. Cutting these online distractions from your workday will make you a more engaged and valuable employee. Ever been in a meeting but not really listening because you were wondering if anything new and interesting had happened online? Or found yourself switching back and forth from work to personal websites, never giving 100 percent to the task at hand? So have the rest of us. Allowing yourself the well-deserved luxury of taking breaks to do nothing—to clear your mind and let it empty of clutter—gives you the power to cut out these online distractions.

If you're struggling to overcome this habit, try this exercise. Write down any moments of procrastination you had at work in the last three days. Try to assign a reason to them, such as avoiding returning an email, stumped on how to finish something, fatigued, or didn't want to start some complicated work. When those same snags slow you down at work in the future, switch from a procrastination activity to a brief break to do nothing.

Prioritize More Effectively

You also get clarity on what your important work is when you do nothing. Sometimes it feels like there's so much to do that it's hard to decide where to start. Everyone wants their work completed yesterday, so it's easy to get bogged down in other people's ideas of what is urgent.

Taking a break to do nothing sends you back to work with clarity on what to prioritize. A study of agricultural and office workers found that a "mindless" break, one where the worker was not engaged in eating, talking to a coworker, or another type of activity, made the worker 15 to 20 percent more effective immediately after returning to work. The researchers' theory is that keeping their minds on standby rather than engaged in activity was the cause of this productivity boost. Breaks that shut out the chatter of life allow you to return to work and hear and see what is truly important in doing your job well. As you practice doing nothing, you get a more peaceful and Zen perspective on what constitutes a true emergency. Most of us aren't working in a hospital emergency room, so "urgency" is a relative thing. Can that job wait until next week or does it have to be done by six o'clock to prevent the sale/project from failing? You'll find the answer to these questions when you take the time to do nothing.

To be competitive in the workplace you need to not only work hard but also work smart. Doing nothing is part of working smart: you can see what the important work is and you can prioritize it in order to do it well.

Do the Hard Work First

"Frog swallowing" is an expression that refers to getting the challenging, difficult, and unpleasant work done first. Understandably, most of us gravitate to doing the easiest tasks first so we can quickly cross them off our list. They're comfortable and don't require us to work outside our comfort zone or the skill set we are best at. They're also often short, easy tasks that we can do without devoting our full attention to them. Many of us start our workday with these tasks, leaving the more daunting tasks for later. Eventually, though, the frog-swallowing tasks build up until there's a pile of unpleasant and demanding work on our plate.

Doing nothing helps you do the hard, frog-swallowing tasks first because you will return to work from your break reenergized and remotivated, ready to tackle a more challenging project. You're even excited about it—you feel momentum to get this difficult task off your plate and show yourself, and your boss, that you can do a great job with it.

Doing nothing is your secret weapon to completing hard work well and on time. You're always going to reply to those easy emails or get that simple work done. But the more challenging tasks aren't always such a given. So, you take the time for a do-nothing break before you begin, and then you tackle the tough work. If you're struggling with a particularly heavy workload or an intense project, don't be afraid to boost the number of your do-nothing breaks. They could be as frequent as twenty minutes of work followed by ten minutes of doing nothing. Set a timer for these intervals, and when your doing-nothing break comes, leave your computer or whatever you're working on behind and go sip your tea while looking out the window or sit in a lotus position on the floor. In the end, even with those breaks, you're likely to get more done and at a higher quality level.

Revamp That Daily Slow Period Into Do-Nothing Time

If you find that you hit a wall at work at the same time every day, your body is trying to tell you something. Embrace your need for a rest at that time, but turn it into a do-nothing break instead of a wasted, frustrating period. For many of us, the majority of our workday and workload isn't flexible. We can't simply do work whenever is best for our inner rhythm. Instead, you can use doing nothing to gain some control over your schedule and work in a way that fits your personality while still aligning with your employer's goals and standards.

A common workday slow period that you can turn around with doing nothing usually occurs in the late afternoon. The caffeine from your morning espresso has burned out of your system, lunch is digesting, and you're close to quitting time...but not so close that you can shut things down. Digging into a larger piece of work seems daunting. It's the perfect time to refresh yourself with fifteen minutes of doing nothing, clearing your mind, and shifting your body. This break to do nothing will give you a burst of energy to dive into a project at the end of the day or finish that lingering work you've been putting off.

Be More Successful at Work

Let's face it: no matter how much you love your job, it's hard to keep yourself motivated and efficient for forty-plus hours a week. Most of us go through periods of happiness in between periods of just getting by and being less than thrilled about going into work. If you're languishing in your job—always feel like you're behind, struggling to find the energy and focus to do great work—doing nothing can help you perform to the best of your abilities because it helps you tap into your natural rhythm of work and rest. Researchers from Florida State University studied the work habits of elite performers (athletes, chess players, and musicians) and found that the best performers typically work in ninety-minute intervals that mimic our natural sleep cycles—the same amount of time it takes to move from light to deep sleep and back out again. These elite performers are so in tune with their bodies that they can feel and know that their best work comes not from hours and hours of continuous practice but from shorter, focused sessions with breaks in between.

The rest of us tend to ignore our physical and mental cues of fatigue or loss of focus and try to power through without breaks, erroneously thinking that more hours equals better work and more success. In fact, this style of long hours and no breaks keeps you out of sync with yourself and prevents you from achieving the success you're after. When you change your style of work and listen to your mental and physical cues of fatigue and lack of focus, you allow yourself to reach your full potential and hit that next level of success in your job. If you're wondering how you're going to get to that next level when you're already working very long days, change up your working style to allow for briefer but more concentrated work sessions with deeply relaxing breaks to do nothing in between.

Doing Nothing Redefines Why You're Working

Why do you work? Sure, everyone needs to pay the bills... But why do you have the job you have? For some people, their job is their passion and a big part of their identity. For others, their job is simply a way to make a living. For some of us, it's a combination of both. No matter where you are on this spectrum, doing nothing will help you remember why you work and give you guidance on how to strategize your career.

Considering Your Future Work Life

Most of us are somewhere in between these two workers: we have an affinity for our work, but we wouldn't do it for free. No matter how much you love your work and how long you have until retirement, the pause of doing nothing can help you find clarity about whether you should pursue advancement in this career or if you are satisfied with your current role. Some of us get so bogged down in our day-to-day routines that we don't stop to consider exactly what our future career plans might be. Doing nothing gives you a clear head to ponder that once in a while. You take those breaks and return to work and really "see" what it is that you do. It's clear what you enjoy about your job (you tend to not need a break when doing it) and what parts you struggle with (you tend to procrastinate around these tasks and take more breaks to do nothing to get them done). It becomes more apparent what you'll need to do to get that next promotion and if you even really want it. You're feeling the positive effects of breaks to do nothing in your personal life, and that gives you space to think about what you want out of your work life. Here are three ways to use the do-nothing philosophy to help identify your career goals:

- **Light:** Imagine doing your same job for the next five years. Are you happy, sad, relieved?
- **Medium:** Think about the next level of your job and what it will take to get there in terms of time, impact to your personal life, and stress.
- **Deep:** Let yourself imagine a dream-job scenario and what it would take to get there. Is it leaving your steady job to freelance, reducing your living expenses so you can work part-time, or going after the more senior role?

Taking the Focus Off Money

Most people think it's a given that they should be working toward increasing their earnings—which usually means working harder and working more hours. After all, making more money should be the goal, right? Make more money so we can buy more stuff and be happier.

Maybe not. It turns out that more money does not always equal more happiness. A 2010 study from Princeton University's Woodrow Wilson School found that happiness increases as income increases up to the point of making $75,000 a year. Once people reach that $75,000 income benchmark, earning more money doesn't bring any greater happiness. We say money can't buy happiness, but really, it can buy *some* happiness. However, that happiness tops out at a certain ceiling.

Taking the time to do nothing gives you an opportunity to mull over exactly what fulfills you and makes you happy. You may find it surprising that making more money isn't actually what will make you happier. Through doing nothing, you'll figure out what activities and people contribute to your overall contentment. The other "things"—more money, more stuff—probably aren't a big part of what makes you feel good daily.

Let's say you've been eyeing that office with an exterior window that comes with your own team to lead and a big raise for three years. The day finally arrives when it's all yours. You're thrilled until a few weeks in...when you realize that you're now working 40 percent more for a 15 percent raise.

It's ingrained in our culture that we should be seeking more money and power. To simply enjoy where you are at is often thought of as being unambitious or lazy. Doing nothing will enlighten you to the radical and life-changing concept that there are positives and negatives to getting promoted.

In addition, responsibility, stress, and work hours are not always proportional to salaries. If you've ever wondered why your colleague, the happy one who everyone likes, has turned down promotions twice, here's her secret: she knows that job titles grow in inverse proportion to personal instability and stress. This life lesson is a hard one to come by, and many people refuse to believe they wouldn't be happier with more responsibility, power, and a higher salary. They think the higher you get, the easier it gets, because more people are "under" you to do the hard work. But that's really not how it works. You have less free time and more pressure to perform at a high level. Some people really do thrive professionally in those situations, and that's where they find true happiness in their life. If that's you, great—just be sure that you arrive at that decision thoughtfully and intentionally, not by blindly following the crowd.

The next step in this process might be realizing that making more money isn't where you want to focus your energy on a daily basis. It's life-changing to figure out that you don't actually want to pursue a bonus or a new job title. Suddenly you're free from the burden of pursuing more money. Doing nothing brings out the joy you find in the simple things in your life, the things that don't really cost much. Once you have that realization, the pursuit of money won't hold the same power over you.

> Doing nothing brings out the joy you find in the simple
> things in your life, the things that don't really cost much.

Many people *want* more money but many of us don't *need* more money. See the difference? When you practice doing nothing regularly, when you have this new peace in your life, you can see that when your basics are covered—shelter, food, clothing—you don't need a lot more to be any happier. Relationships and activities become much more fulfilling when we are doing nothing because we learn how to give them our full attention. The shopping for fun, buying stuff just out of habit or because it once felt good, falls by the wayside.

Stepping out of the constant quest for more money lets you:

- De-stress and simply enjoy your work more.
- See that you don't want to hunger after more money, accolades, and promotions.

- Focus on just enjoying the work you do and taking pride in it.
- Become less concerned with big-picture results and more concerned with process, enjoying the work for the work's sake instead of as a path to the next promotion or raise.

Ironically, deciding to just enjoy your job and not worry about money and advancement can lead to more money and advancement because it encourages the kind of earnest and engaged work that results in recognition from your boss.

Fall in Love (Again) with Your Job

Doing nothing can help you fall in love with your job all over again. The increased focus and motivation from taking those do-nothing breaks can help you find the parts and perks of your job that you enjoy most and lead you to focus your energy on them. It's like starting a new career or taking a new job or position without any of the stress or hassle. In Kerry Hannon's book *Love Your Job: The New Rules for Career Happiness*, Hannon outlines many strategies for enjoying your job more, including:

- **Find what you like about your job.** This is something that taking breaks to do nothing can clarify: what part(s) of your job do you return to work energized and looking forward to? Once you know what you like about your job, aim to do more of it. If you like things outside of your actual job—great coworkers, good vacation time, great health coverage—focus your thoughts on those job perks.
- **Declutter your office space.** Hannon says that people often feel low on energy at work because they haven't spent time clearing

things up physically and virtually. When you take a quick break to do nothing, come back to your work and spend a few minutes on those small administrative and paper tasks that tend to build up over time. You'll feel better about yourself and your job when you don't have them hanging over your head.

- **Explore finding joy in the social side of work.** Join the work softball team or volunteer for an event your company supports. Join an employee committee around office recycling, employee fitness, or event planning. Those restorative breaks to do nothing can give you that extra energy to join in when, in the past, you would have said you needed a break from anything affiliated with work. Embracing social and volunteer opportunities through your workplace give new meaning and fulfillment to your job. You'll get to know coworkers in a new way and bond with them over a shared experience. This positive experience related to work will soften any negative feelings about parts of your job you don't enjoy. You will associate work with new and good things in your life.

Use the Do-Nothing Philosophy to Reshape How You Work

Beyond actually taking breaks to do nothing, embracing the philosophy of doing nothing—that deep rest is necessary and a powerful tool—can reshape how you work. We've talked about the direct benefits of these restorative breaks on your career and workdays, but there are more ways that the ethos of doing nothing can positively impact your work life.

Separate Your Work and Personal Life

Doing nothing is a great path to work/life balance. If you're very passionate about your job, you might become so engaged that you forget to also prioritize your personal life. Doing nothing will help you take a small step back and take care of your physical and emotional well-being, creating a more balanced life. You'll start to think of work as a break from the rest of your life and the rest of your life as a break from work. Your focus will be whole and on task. Taking those breaks to do nothing at the beginning and end of your workday will help you release any work/life stress or lingering thoughts.

Doing nothing also helps you separate your work life and personal life because it empowers you to stay completely focused on what's in front of you. You're able to forget about work demands when at home and forget about personal demands at work. This is an incredibly useful skill to develop because round-the-clock availability and high work stress can make it challenging to be focused on home life at home and work life at work. Taking breaks at work and at home to release any stress allows you to stay in the moment and focus your attention on the important people and work in your life.

Set Boundaries

Doing nothing helps you set boundaries in today's 24/7 work world. You'll be able to say no to work easily when you're off the clock because you'll know that you're already working hard when you're officially on the job. You'll also recognize that your life outside of work is just as, if not more, important to you. When your mind is open to the idea that too much work and burnout is *optional*, you'll understand your choices: you can switch jobs, or you can tell your manager you no longer want overtime. You have agency over your time. This is also the golden rule that applies to finding moments to unwind and do nothing: make your time your own.

The more you make time for doing nothing, the easier setting boundaries becomes. Doing nothing frees your mind of work and personal life burdens. This distance from troubles big and small makes them more manageable. Those big problems that were running through your head all day change into small hurdles that will work themselves out. This clear perspective gives you the strength to set boundaries—like telling your boss you can't stay late or letting the manager know she must call in another employee to cover breaks during an unusually busy day. It's just work. Unless you're literally giving someone CPR, it's not life or death. Repeat that mantra.

Give Realistic Timelines

You start to see how long work tasks actually take when you're regularly taking breaks to do nothing. You know what your true work speed is (not your imagined or hoped-for speed) and can work at that true and optimum pace, planning your tasks accordingly. That means you can start to give realistic timelines about when your work will be complete—a skill most people need to work on.

Setting realistic work goals also provides more opportunities for those valuable do-nothing breaks. Brief and restorative meditation time is easier to squeeze in when you're not overworked or behind on a deadline. You're working efficiently and staying focused, you've given yourself a competitive but reasonable amount of time to complete your work, and you have ten minutes to clear your mind, relax your body, and do nothing.

Learn to Say No More

*When you say "yes" to others, make sure
you are not saying "no" to yourself.*
—Paulo Coelho, Author

Getting comfortable saying no more is just as important in your work life as it is in your everyday life. Doing nothing makes you:

- Confident, because you are doing your best work.
- Calmer, so you don't reflexively say yes to every request. You pause, and if need be, you tell the other person that you'll get back to them on that.
- Aware that you don't need to say yes to everything to be a content, fulfilled, and productive employee.
- Value your time. You can see what you give to your job, and you can see where the line is between your job and your interests and commitments in the rest of your life.
- Give a decisive and humble response. Saying no is also a gift. You're letting that person move on and get what they need elsewhere. You've got the humility and confidence to know that you're not the only one that can get the job done.

Saying no protects your do-nothing time. The time you make to do nothing gives back to you (and your employer) exponentially in focus and ideas. Remember this when you decline to take those extra tables during the lunch rush or when you firmly tell your coworker you can't format their documents for them. Saying no to extra work means saying yes to higher quality work and better engagement by doing nothing. Here are three examples of ways to say no at work:

- **Light:** Skip the after-work drinks that you always feel obligated to go to (during which you always watch the clock until you feel you can safely leave without being noticed). Simply say you have other plans (even if those plans are doing nothing!).
- **Medium:** Say no to work that's outside of your job description and that impacts you negatively (keeps you late, makes your other work suffer). If you are repeatedly asked to do work that's outside of your role—either above your pay grade or work for another department—set some boundaries by saying no.
- **Deep:** Say no to a promotion if you know it's not the right role for you to take. It takes a happy and calm soul to say no to advancement, but if you know it's not the right time or right role for you, politely decline.

Want to effortlessly say no to planning a retirement lunch for a coworker you've only said hi to once or cleanly remove yourself as a candidate for the boss's new pet project? The following are a few ways to say no politely and firmly.

- "I'm afraid I've got my plate full with _____ (current projects) but I appreciate you considering me for this project."

- "While it sounds interesting, I don't have much experience in _____ , so I won't be much help."

- "That's not my area of expertise, but I know _____ (coworker) has a lot of knowledge in that area."
- "With my current workload, I wouldn't be able to get that work back to you for a number of (days, weeks). If you need it done right away, I'm afraid I can't help."

Finding the Time to Do Nothing at Work

Some workplaces require more discretion and creativity to make doing nothing a part of your workday. You'll have to recognize what works for you and for your office or work culture. You may need to set your work line to go straight to voice mail for a short time, log out of your computer, or even put headphones on so people don't disturb you. No matter what your job, there truly is time to take a restorative break to do nothing at work.

Work Within the Structure and Culture of Your Job

Every workplace is different in both physical location and space, time demands, and culture. A salesperson who spends most of his or her time visiting clients has a different set of challenges and opportunities related to finding time and space to do nothing compared to a fourth-grade teacher.

A tenet to remember as you search for this time and space: no one is watching you as closely as you watch yourself. For instance, can you remember what a coworker wore to work last Monday? Or (if setting lunch break hours are up to individual employees), do you make a note each day of when people went on lunch and when they came back? Do you know how often most people in your office use the bathroom or wander to the vending machines for a midmorning snack and some office gossip? Take comfort and confidence in the fact that most of us are too busy focusing on our own lives and work to worry, wonder, or make note of what the person next to us is doing.

One truth to almost every workplace: people already take the time to do nothing. It may be under the cover of longer breaks or procrastination, but it's happening. The big difference between them and you is that you're going to make your do-nothing time matter. Instead of wasting time, you'll intentionally do nothing to bring more joy to your day and to refresh yourself for more productive and creative work. Here are three recommendations for adjusting your do-nothing breaks to the culture of your job:

- **Light:** For the conservative workplace, help your do-nothing time blend in by taking it during a standard break and pretending to read a book with headphones on. No one will interrupt you or realize that you're actually doing completely and utterly nothing.
- **Medium:** If your workplace supports injury-preventing stretch breaks, use a few laps around the office as your do-nothing time.
- **Deep:** If your workplace already has a meditation room that everyone is encouraged to use, you're set! Take advantage of this quiet space to sit in silence and let your mind go blank.

The Do-Nothing Pause Before or after Work

Think about your routine before you start work. Do you warm your-self up before you start big and challenging tasks, or do you dive in to the really hard work from a cold start? Most of us ease into work, grabbing a cup of coffee, checking our email, maybe browsing some news sites, and then, thirty minutes after we've arrived at work, we get down to business. Likewise, at the end of your workday, do you work feverishly right up until you grab your jacket and head out the door or do you wind things down slowly, closing programs as you finish tasks or completing an end-of-day routine? Most of us naturally have a wind up and wind down to our workday or work shift. These warm-ups or cooldowns at the start and end of our workday are ideal for a pause to do nothing.

Make the pause for doing nothing a part of your warm-up and cool-down for the workday. Before you open your email program or after you pour yourself a cup of coffee, take even just three minutes to sit calmly, breathe deeply, and empty your mind of any worries or nagging thoughts. Make it as much a part of your day as logging out of your computer or flipping the "open" sign on the shop door to "closed." If you need to be on duty right away, arrive ten minutes early and do nothing before you step in to work. Take another ten minutes once you are off your shift and before you leave work. Be intentional—no distractions!—and remind yourself of the value of those minutes to both your work and the rest of your life. Taking those moments of quiet first thing will focus you for the long day ahead. Later, time spent doing nothing at the end of the workday will let you release any tension or niggling work thoughts and allow you to start enjoying your life off the clock as soon as you walk out the door.

Here's a useful exercise: write down your work and personal hours for the week. Add in a short break to do nothing that will transition you from work to personal time and personal time to work. This will be easy if you work shifts or have very defined hours. If you work flexible hours throughout the day, start keeping a daily time journal. Seeing your days and hours mapped out will give you a motivating and clear picture of how much time you have to yourself and where you can fit doing nothing into your schedule.

Setting Your Work Hours for More Time to Do Nothing

The steady predictability of working nine to five in an office is a thing of the past. We are working at home, in the car, on vacation, and even from our phones as we shop for groceries. This change in when we work is an opportunity to create the ideal schedule that allows for pockets of time to reset and rest with doing nothing.

If you have any flexibility in your schedule, you can make more time to do nothing by working within your most productive hours. Traditional office hours don't take into account that people work differently:

- Some of us do our most productive work in the early morning.
- Others need a slow and relaxed beginning to the day before they can engage themselves in work and hit their stride right at midday.
- Night owls find themselves in the zone when the sun sets and work deep into the night.

We are not the same, yet we're all expected to work at the same time. If at all possible, you should work when you're most productive.

Give your best when your brain and body feel their best. Rest and do nothing when your energy is low and you're at your least productive. This guiding principle should be used to set your work hours.

Now, is it possible for the night owl to work four o'clock to midnight when he or she must meet with clients, discuss projects with coworkers, and collaborate with a team? Is it possible for the night owl to awake at ten o'clock, ease into the day with light activity and breakfast, meet with friends, and then take an hour to do nothing before starting her workday as most of the city is ending theirs? Maybe not. But night owls could adjust their workday to get some of their work done in their peak performance window and take time to do nothing in their slow and less productive window. This simple concept of working in your productive window will guide you in maximizing both your work and your time doing nothing. Here are three prospective options for changing your work schedule to fit your productivity windows:

- **Light:** Ask if you can start your workday earlier once a week to hit your early-morning productivity sweet spot. Most employers are amenable to a small change in schedule.
- **Medium:** Ask to telecommute one or two days a week. This allows for greater flexibility for those who do their best work outside of the regular nine-to-five office hours.
- **Deep:** Become a contractor or freelancer, work from home, and set your own schedule. The reduced job security could be balanced out with more productivity from working the hours that suit you best.

Negotiate Flexible Work Hours for More Time to Do Nothing

Here are a few ideas for starting that delicate conversation with your manager about flexible work hours:

- Say something like, "I would like to shift my start time and finish time to work within the hours I am most productive. I will still be here for the core hours of the workday but will start/finish earlier/later. Should a meeting happen outside of my hours, I will shift my start/finish time for that day."
- If you have a manager that's skeptical of flexible work hours, ask for a trial period. During that trial period, make sure your work is impeccable and keep notes on the results. Present these results at the end of the trial period and ask for a long-term shift in your hours. The rewards of the time you take to do nothing, your productivity, and the quality of your work will speak volumes about the benefit of shifting your schedule to take breaks to do nothing.
- If you work in shifts and your role is responsive (you provide services and coverage during a set window of time, for instance), you probably won't have much flexibility to set your hours. But that isn't necessarily all bad. The positive to not having flexible work hours is predictability. You always know when you're working. Use this to your advantage by mapping out your time to do nothing alongside your work schedule. If you already know your work hours for the next six months, you can also plan your do-nothing time that far in advance as well. And planning well in advance, knowing that you have a lot of time to do nothing and that there are a series of reminders in your calendar prompting you to do just that, ensures that you will take that time for yourself.

Finding the Space to Do Nothing at Work

Is it possible to sit quietly for twenty minutes doing nothing where you work or is there simply too much going on around you? You may need to find a hideaway within the building or even step outside to take this time to yourself. For physical space, you want to find a spot that's reliable and somewhat private. *Reliable* meaning it doesn't move around or get booked up and *private* meaning it's not on display to customers or in the line of fire from coworkers looking for resources or help. If there aren't any safe places to joyously do nothing at your place of work, you can aim to do nothing under the guise of performing another task. If your job involves light manual labor, look to those times when you're doing a task that is repetitive and doesn't require much focus to take a mental break and do nothing.

Start Simple with Your Physical Location

Your do-nothing spot could be as simple as your desk. You could put on some noise-canceling headphones and meditate for fifteen minutes without tipping off your coworkers. If people try to get your attention with the headphones on, try opening a book or gazing vacantly at some other paper reading material. You want to look busy without engaging in work. It's a fine balance to master.

The other obvious spot for a secret do-nothing break: the bathroom. Leave that magazine and your phone behind when you are in the bathroom. Enjoy that break from work and thinking and being busy. If you're laughing at this suggestion, good! You need to see the possibility of doing nothing in any of the regular and mundane daily tasks that fill your life. Even the ones involving toilets.

Change Your Surroundings

Beyond the usual nooks and spare offices and break rooms, look to change your surroundings for a do-nothing break when you can. If you work outdoors, find a way to go inside for a short do-nothing break. If you work indoors, take the time to get outside—even if the surroundings are less than beautiful. Even just standing outside staring at the parking lot or walking around the office building a few times will take your mind and body away from work. This change of air and surroundings is a great method for getting into your do-nothing time if you find it hard to mentally and physically escape your work. You're also less likely to get interrupted during your do-nothing time if you physically step away from where your work happens.

Find Mental Space

If you need to make your do-nothing time work while performing some light manual labor, consider how you will make that work as a mental break when it's not a physical break. If you normally listen to music or the radio while doing this type of work (organizing a supply closet, for example), do the work in silence. Let your mind empty. Don't think ahead to what the next task is or what you should make for dinner. Enjoy the quiet of the space you're in and that you don't have to worry or think about anything other than the simple task at hand. Look at this job as a gift, a break from the rest of your day and time to shut out the rest of the world, people, places, text messages, talk radio, and any stresses that are lingering in your mind.

Finding Space Before and after Work

Some people enjoy a do-nothing break before they begin their day. If you won't be left alone to do nothing in your workplace before you start work, find an alternative spot. It could be sitting in your car in the parking lot or discreetly in the lobby of your building. Yes, it could be the bathroom. If you need to be visually out of sight to prevent coworkers and managers engaging with you before the start of your workday, you may need to do nothing in some unusual places. It could be an empty boardroom or supply closet. It could be at your desk with a headset on, pretending you are listening in on a meeting.

Try a Variety of Things

There will be trial and error to finding just the right space and time for doing nothing. The camouflage of pretending to be on a call may work one day and not the next. Remind yourself that even five minutes of time to do nothing will relax your mind and body and set you up for a great day of work or infuse focus into your post-work plans. Just like an athlete, you need a warm-up and a cooldown from your work, and a do-nothing pause does just that.

Remember, you really can do nothing anywhere at (almost) any time. Work is no exception. You can, and will, get your do-nothing time in even if you don't have a private office. Use your surroundings, break rooms, desk, or your trusty standby—the bathroom—to get your do-nothing time in at work.

Maximizing Your Breaks to Do Nothing

Some work is so demanding that there is no way to safely take a mental and physical break while on the job. The job is intense and requires all your capacities for the duration of your work hours. Maybe you work with patients, perform detailed and painstaking work, or are part of a team that requires all its members be completely engaged at all times in the task at hand. Letting your mind slip away to do nothing while on a job like this could be dangerous or just impossible. There's no room to leave work at a standstill for a quick moment of doing nothing. In this case, use your breaks to their maximum.

Take Your Break. Really.

One way to find the time to do nothing at work: take your break. It's common for employees with high-stress, client-focused jobs to skip breaks because their workload is so high stakes. At times this is just unavoidable—you simply must skip the standard breaks due to the nature of your work. But remember, those breaks are there for a reason! Experts know you need them. Workers in potentially dangerous industries like truck driving have federal laws that require them to rest. In fact, drivers of commercial and freight vehicles have to take a ten-hour break after eleven hours of work. For workers in other industries, some states have rest and lunch break policies that companies must adhere to. According to Stanford University, taking frequent short breaks has been shown to reduce employee burnout and increase job satisfaction. All the more reason to take that break.

Most companies will have a written policy on break frequency and what breaks are paid or unpaid. Check with your human resources department to find out the exact policy at your company. Try to take whatever break you are entitled to, and remind yourself that it's not only good for your own health but also good for the company.

Sometimes you can manage to take a break by being persistent. Ask your manager to call in extra staff or notify clients there will be a slight delay in service. If your earnings are a fee for service and the amount of work you do for your clients determines how much you earn, be wary of the trap of not taking breaks to earn a little more. Not taking proper rest away from your work will burn you out and eventually impact your earnings even more. Think of a break to do nothing as future earnings; you're taking care of yourself so you can continue to do your job well. Here are three strategies for fitting breaks into your workday:

- **Light:** Set an alarm to remind yourself to take a midmorning break. It doesn't have to be long—even just five minutes to stretch, move, and clear your mind is a great start to prioritizing breaks.
- **Medium:** Say no to working through or skipping lunch. Even if you can only squeeze in twenty minutes, commit to setting work aside, clearing your mind, and nourishing yourself.
- **Deep:** Put two daily recurring fifteen-minute breaks into your work calendar. Try not to accept meetings during this time or, if you have to, reschedule your break for another time that day. Make taking your breaks a priority for your work performance and health.

Make Your Break Count

Make the breaks you do take as refreshing and restorative as possible. It's so easy to step away from your intense job and go to those easy distractions—caffeine, sugar, gossip, screens—to get a break. But if you use your breaks to distract yourself, you rarely come back refreshed. Flipping through your phone for fifteen minutes isn't restorative, nor is wolfing down a chocolate bar while commiserating about the struggles of your job with a coworker.

That's why it's so important to get your do-nothing time in—you really need the joy of doing nothing to balance your demanding work. Set aside one break a day to step away from the thoughts and busyness of your work and joyfully do nothing. This break will not only help you focus more when you resume work, but it will also give you a positive feeling from doing something just for yourself during your busy day. So, when you do get the chance to put your work down, let yourself slip into the blissful state of doing nothing. Here is some guidance on how to make your break as restorative as possible:

- **Light:** Become a tea drinker. That's right, use the meditative and nourishing ritual of boiling water and brewing tea to make your break feel restful and restorative.
- **Medium:** Get out of the office or workplace. Make a habit of getting a change of scenery once a day for a short break, even if it's just stepping outside for ten minutes.
- **Deep:** Leave your personal cell phone at home during the work-day. Bring a book as entertainment, if needed, but mostly use your breaks to reboot your brain with doing nothing.

Take a Day Off from Work to Do Nothing

Take a day off from work at least once a year to do nothing. No, this isn't a sick day spent in bed, replying to urgent work emails in between rounds of naps and cough syrup. This also isn't a day used to play catch-up on the rest of your life: no dentist appointments or painting your bathroom or unpacking boxes from your recent move. This is a day of wellness just for you. This is a day to do anything and everything at your whim. It could be a solo dining experience sandwiched in between watching a movie trilogy. Whatever it is, make it something indulgent and out of the ordinary, restful, and relaxing.

• • •

As you've seen, there are so many ways to do nothing at work so you can be a happier, more productive, and engaged employee. The wonder of doing nothing, how it resets your mind and gives you another level of focus and energy, is a great tool to manage your energy throughout the workday. Doing nothing can bring those creative ideas you need and that afternoon energy you're missing. Doing nothing can also help you see what you really want to get out of your work: a paycheck, fulfillment, or advancement. And having a clear objective in mind with your work, one you find and shape through regular do-nothing breaks, makes for a more enjoyable workday and helps you achieve work-life balance.

Home

He is happiest, be he king or peasant,
who finds peace in his home.
—Johann Wolfgang von Goethe, Poet and Philosopher

Your home is your sanctuary and one of the best places to make a habit of doing nothing. In this chapter, we'll explore the act of doing nothing at home—how to block out any chatter and how to make it part of your home routine. You'll also learn how to create a space that encourages and allows you to do nothing in peace. A busy household humming with activity is a joy in itself—and it won't prevent you from finding time and space to do nothing. Your home is your castle, and when you're doing nothing, you want that space to give you maximum refreshment per minute.

Any home can be easily transformed into the ideal space to do nothing. This change won't require new furniture or moving or getting new roommates. You can simply work with what you've got to create a peaceful environment to do nothing in for ten minutes or even a whole day. Yelping dogs, new babies, and loud roommates are no match for your personalized plan to find time and space to relax, listen to the breeze rustle a curtain, and let any worries or stress disappear.

Doing Nothing with Other People Around

If you live alone in a soundproof home, you can skip this section of the book: you've already got an easy setup for doing nothing at home. However, if like most people you have roommates, loud neighbors, or a family, you'll want to use this section to help you find the right time and space to do nothing at home.

Home represents some of the best aspects of your life—your family, your belongings, your treasured memories. Remember, one of the reasons you're doing nothing is to relax and enjoy the important things in your life more. Enjoying life more includes savoring and strengthening your relationships with the people you live with. This section will help you strike a balance in meeting your needs while also being respectful of the needs of others in your household.

Find a Do-Nothing Spot

You likely already have a favorite spot at home that you retreat to for quiet, thoughtful work. It could be one end of the couch, your desk, or the swing on your porch. Try to designate a space where you can retreat to most of the time, no matter the time of day or the weather. If you have roommates, it may simply be the center of the rug in your bedroom, sitting lotus-style with a few throw pillows around you, or for more back support, sitting on the floor with your back against the wall. Try and remove yourself from the usual traffic patterns of your housemates. The following are some other factors to consider as you choose a place to do nothing.

A Stress-Free Spot

Identify where you feel most comfortable. This means both mentally and physically comfortable, so avoid hard chairs or awkward spaces. Try not to take your do-nothing time into spaces where you normally do heavy work. If your home office is filled with unfinished tax forms or other paperwork on your to-do list, and the garage is home to many half-completed home projects, avoid those areas. You want to easily slip into your do-nothing time without being reminded of work that hasn't been done or should be done or that you really don't want to do. Remember, this is your time to let all of those thoughts go away so you can replenish yourself and truly relax.

Fresh Air

If you can, choose a space that has access to the outdoors. Fresh air will help transport you into a calm and relaxed state when you do nothing. You want to feel like you're stepping outside of your routine when you do nothing, and a change in air temperature, along with the smells and sounds of the outdoors, can give you that change. It doesn't even have to be a typical outdoor space. Simply being able to open a window or door is enough to get that refreshed feeling.

Noise Levels

Once you find your spot, try to determine if you hear noise that could hinder your relaxation time. You want to give yourself a calm and quiet corner that lets you easily slip into doing nothing. If your front room has wonderful light but faces a noisy and high-traffic street, find a quieter spot. Some outside noise is almost unavoidable, so don't worry if you live in a noisy and less-than-soundproofed home. If it truly isn't possible to find a quiet space, don't worry. Over time, you will learn to block out those noises and distractions while you do nothing. You really can do nothing from any place at any time.

If you have young kids, excitable dogs, or a never-empty-of-people living room, it may seem like there are no pockets or corners of quiet in your household. If you can't go to the bathroom without being interrupted, you're living in a busy (and hopefully fun) household. Like those with very busy schedules, people with busy homes have to use a bit of creativity and rely on those fringe hours to find their ideal do-nothing space and time.

Work Around the Rhythm of the Household

You'll want to get your do-nothing time in when it doesn't conflict with household routines and activities. When is your quiet corner for doing nothing busy? When is your household awake and loud and wanting to engage with you? You may find that your do-nothing time is best arranged outside of the normal household hours and activities:

- Maybe you wake up fifteen minutes before everyone else or stay up a little later to get that calm and quiet space and time.
- Or, you might incorporate your pause to do nothing in the transition time between the evening meal and evening activities.

Be Flexible with Your Do-Nothing Time

If you live in a busy household, you may not be able to practice your do-nothing time consistently in your ideal window. For example:

- Night owls who want to chill out late into the evening may have roommates up who want to chat with them or coerce them into watching television, taking up their little corner of peace and quiet.
- Parents may have babies up in the middle of the night.
- Some of us must check in with our jobs outside of office hours.

Don't fret. Instead, be flexible. Find little windows of time that might otherwise go unused—those are perfect for restorative do-nothing time.

If you need to shift your do-nothing time, reimagine time you're already spending sitting or waiting, such as:

- Have some zone-out do-nothing time on the train in to work or while standing in line at the coffee shop.
- If you've just rocked a baby to sleep, sit there for an extra five minutes, slumbering child in your arms, and let your mind empty for a quick do-nothing break.
- Find your do-nothing escape while you do the dishes. Leave the radio off and free your mind of any stresses or worry.
- Take a break...in your car. If you drive home and are alone in your car (or have sleeping children/calm dogs) with you, take your do-nothing time in your car.
- Say yes to chores that give you alone time. Then take five for a do-nothing break before you start folding laundry or making beds or mowing the lawn.
- Practice doing nothing within the noise and activity of your home. Find that silence in your mind by ignoring the cacophony around you. Fake that you're taking a nap on the couch when really, you're awake and resting your mind and body.

- Take your do-nothing time when most of your household is engaged in an activity. That could mean shifting when you eat dinner or breakfast or excusing yourself from the evening board game. When everyone is doing something, take your time to do nothing.

Be patient and watchful, and the day will present you with an opportunity to get your do-nothing time in—though maybe not the one you first had in mind.

Invite Your Roommates or Family Along

An easy way to make doing nothing at home possible: invite your family or roommates along. Sharing the joy of doing nothing makes for an easy, exponentially joyful habit. It's also a great strategy for finding the time and space in a busy household for your own do-nothing time. Your housemates will finally understand the appeal of doing nothing, and you'll all reap the benefits.

The rewards of having your roommates do nothing with you are many:

- You'll bond over the rejuvenating experience of doing nothing.
- Your household will be calmer and more harmonious.
- Finding the time and space to do nothing won't be a problem: your household will be in tune with and respectful about your time to do nothing.
- Spreading the joy of doing nothing to others creates a ripple effect, and their positivity and joyfulness will touch others. You're doing your entire community a favor when you invite others to do nothing.

How do you bring up doing nothing with your roommates? It's easy. Here are a few examples of how to broach the subject.

- "I thought tonight we could leave the television off and just relax together. Any takers?"
- "Can we try our morning routine with the music off and some quiet?"
- "I'd love to really relax, wouldn't you? We can put all the electronic devices away for an hour and just enjoy some silence together."

It may take a few tries for your housemates or family to catch on to your suggestions. Modeling the benefits of doing nothing can provide better engagement on the topic with others, and the complete focus you can give to tasks and people as a result of do-nothing breaks will be another form of encouragement for them. Be patient. They will come around when the time is right for them. Here are three strategies for asking housemates or family to bring the joy of doing nothing into your home:

- **Light:** Ask if you can have one evening a week reserved for quiet with no television on and no guests or hosting.
- **Medium:** Pamper your housemates with an afternoon of rest. Ask everyone to get any work or household chores completed in the morning and then have a full afternoon of rest together. Put out some light reading options (like magazines), some easy and delicious snacks, and urge your family or friends to kick back and do almost nothing with you.
- **Deep:** Take a secular Sabbath once a week together. Tailor it to work with everyone's schedule but aim for a lofty goal of almost a

full day of rest. Make your own rules for it, such as staying offline, no turning the stove on, or spending most of the day in nature.

Designing a Space to Do Nothing

Your home can actually help you do nothing. That's right, you can create an inviting space to relax, shut out the world, and reset your mind and body. It's not just the rhythm or schedule or noise of your household that facilitates quiet and restorative moments but also how your rooms are furnished and designed. Creating more white space, removing obstacles to finding quiet, and making your home an oasis and refuge in a busy life will help you do nothing easily and regularly.

You don't need a specific type of home or any expensive materials to shape a do-nothing area. It will work in a five-bedroom house or a studio apartment. It can be shared space or just yours alone. You can live in the country or the city. All you need to make a comfortable space to do nothing in is a bit of time and an openness to try some new things. No trips to IKEA or investing in art or décor needed.

What Is White Space?

White space is a term originally used in design and art to describe the space unmarked by text, graphics, or objects. Sometimes it is called negative space, meaning an absence of something. The term has transcended design to describe both physical white space and space in your daily life, like your schedule or routines. When you think of creating a space in your home to do nothing, or making your home a place that encourages you to take that time to yourself, think of white space as the absence of furniture, clutter, or décor.

Why Do We Need More White Space?

Blocking out distractions will really facilitate your ability to do nothing. Creating more white space in your home—a streamlined bookshelf that doesn't distract you with clutter, or a living room that allows you to access a healthy amount of floor space—helps you seamlessly and regularly slip into doing nothing.

For some of us, the challenge of blocking out your surroundings actually creates more work. (I need to clean up that laundry on the floor.) It might even prevent you from doing nothing regularly and getting the full benefit of this time to yourself! It's no surprise so many of us struggle with feeling overwhelmed with our homes and our stuff: according to AEIdeas, today's homes are 1,000 square feet larger than they were forty years ago, and living space per person has almost doubled in that time. All that space we have gives us more license to accumulate stuff, and that stuff creates a lot of stress. A study from the Princeton University Neuroscience Institute showed that clutter visually competes for your attention and wears down your ability to focus. When you create more white space in your home, it not only makes it more livable, but it also encourages you to take that sweet time to do nothing that's so vital to our health, happiness, and wellness.

How to Create More White Space

Take a quick survey of your home: what distracts you consciously or unconsciously?

- Do you have all of your mail, opened and unopened, sitting in a central, highly visible location? Do you see that stack of mail, the work it represents to file it, and feel stress from it?
- Is there an end table that you, and everyone else in your home, constantly bump into?
- Have the kids' toys and belongings crept into every room in the house?

Small things like this, things you see as innocuous, can often distract you, raise your stress level, and prevent you from fully engaging in your do-nothing time.

Creating more white space in your home to help you do nothing is easy. You don't have to go buy anything or search endlessly for the perfect throw cushion. You simply need to remove some of the unnecessary. Trim what you already have, move a few things to another room, and unearth a few square feet of livable and open space in your home. If your home is already spartanly furnished, or you've been meaning to add more to it, you're probably already done. Just resist adding more.

If you need to edit what you already have to get more white space, here are a few ideas:

- **Remove 10 percent.** That's right, just take out a small piece of furniture and an armful of décor. See how calm and inviting your space feels with a fraction of less stuff in it. Take the removed items to another room or to storage at first if it makes you more comfortable. Don't worry about getting rid of things permanently. Just put a few things out of sight and mind to try on how the room feels.

- **For the boisterously decorated and colorful home, create one corner or room with extra white space.** See how that space feels and how it attracts you over time.
- **Consider what pieces of furniture get used with the highest frequency and what pieces are ornamental or rarely used.** If you're not using it, try living without it.
- **Try to rearrange with beautiful and peaceful sight lines in mind.** Make that view from your do-nothing armchair beautiful and inviting. Sit there, see what your view is like, and make any necessary alterations.
- **Edit your high-traffic areas for less congestion.** It could be rolling up that hallway rug everyone trips on, pushing a couch a few feet in one direction, or getting rid of the coat rack that only ever holds one coat. Make it easy to move in your home.

Creating more white space in your home allows you to slip into your do-nothing time easily and quickly. Less stuff tripping you up or blocking your calm view will help you get the most out of your do-nothing time.

The Blank Refrigerator

In the book *Life at Home in the Twenty-First Century: 32 Families Open Their Doors*, researchers from the University of California, Los Angeles, studied thirty-two middle-class, dual-income families. Among their shocking findings about how we spend our time and fill our space was that the number of items on a family's refrigerator corresponded to the amount of clutter and consumer goods in the home. The study also related higher stress levels to higher clutter.

Your takeaway from this: clear the front and sides of your refrigerator of clutter. Leave just a few special and current items on your refrigerator and get into the habit of filing and putting away things you would normally post there. Make this small change and see the ripple effect of creating a calm and inviting space. Your clear and tidy refrigerator will be a signal to you and further encouragement to make the time to do nothing.

Benefits of a Do-Nothing Household

Making your home an easy place to do nothing will also help you simplify your household routines and chores. Think about the time you spend each day keeping your home running smoothly, wiping down surfaces, clearing all the small items that accumulate in the wrong place each day, and performing the usual routines of meals and laundry. Then there are the bigger monthly or semiannual tasks of home upkeep, like seasonal chores. Wouldn't it be wonderful to easily and simply cut these chores down while still maintaining a comfortable and clean home? You can do all those things when you get into the mindset of joyfully doing nothing.

- **Doing nothing makes no mess.** There's something really beautiful about a rejuvenating activity that is basically zero emission, zero garbage, and totally free. When you make a habit of taking time to do nothing, you'll naturally create less mess to clean up.
- **You'll find yourself drawn away from buying things you don't really need.** So much of household work now is time spent cleaning up,

organizing, and maintaining stuff (most of which we don't often use). Once you're in the habit of joyfully doing nothing regularly, you'll naturally find yourself with less to clean up, look after, and tidy.

- **Uninterrupted time to relax leaves you with clarity about what's important.** That includes knowing what the important tasks are around your house. You'll find yourself easily prioritizing what needs to be done right away and what can wait.
- **You'll see unnecessary or complicated tasks in a new light.** You'll take a new tack with those tasks and outsource them or change when you do them (so you have more energy for the work) or simply decide that the work of maintaining that thing isn't worth keeping it.
- **Your more mundane tasks can turn into joyful do-nothing time.** Where once you may have bemoaned the twenty minutes it takes to wipe out your refrigerator, you now look forward to it: the work is so easy that you can complete it while enjoying some quiet time to yourself. You may even find yourself looking forward to or volunteering for chores you once avoided.

You can see now that you can take some personal quiet time, uninterrupted by anyone or anything, while you get those simple household tasks done. Doing nothing can actually help you get some things done.

Simplify Household Tasks When You Do Nothing

Have you ever spent an hour cleaning or tidying only to feel that you didn't make any difference to the state of your home? We often get distracted by household work that doesn't give us any return on investment. Sadly, our time seems to evaporate with no great results. The good news: you can easily change this by prioritizing and simplifying household tasks. And doing nothing will help you have fresh eyes for what's important and help you easily decide what stays, what goes, and what can be done differently.

Do the Tasks You Usually Avoid First Instead

Do you gravitate to detailed but not totally necessary household work? Are you quick to do the easiest tasks first? One way to take a new look at your household tasks is to break out of your usual routine and start with the tasks you tend to leave for last. It's that same "frog swallowing" idea we talked about in the Work chapter of this book. Do those items that are out of your wheelhouse first when you have energy and focus for them after taking a break to do nothing.

Eliminate Tasks Altogether

Give up some of your tasks that aren't giving back to you. This could be as simple as not folding laundry. If you have children, do a test run of just laying clothing in drawers instead of folding them first. If adult clothing can be put away without folding, put that on your easy, do-nothing household management list as well. It may seem small, but saving thirty minutes a week not folding clothes will give back to you in so many ways: less stress and more time to do nothing.

Outsource

Another option to eliminate tasks: outsource. Getting household help, for example, a biweekly cleaner, or help with home and yard maintenance, can reduce a lot of stress. Many families spend their weekends checking off household work they simply don't have time to get done during the week. There's little time for hobbies, relaxing together, or doing nothing when the lawn needs to be mowed, gutters repaired, and the kitchen is long overdue for a deep clean. If you can find room in your budget, outsourcing tasks can open up hours of time and relieve significant stress.

> If you can find room in your budget, outsourcing tasks can open up hours of time and relieve significant stress.

Outsourcing can also help you spend less in other areas, allowing you to cook at home more, for instance, and reduced stress will help you resist impulse purchases. Think of the investment in outsourcing as an investment in your health and happiness: less stress and more time for doing nothing and anything else that makes you feel great.

Make a Not-to-Do List

This is a list of things you're going to commit to not doing and not thinking about so that you have more time and energy for yourself and for things like doing nothing. What's on a "not-to-do" list? Tasks that either take up more time than they are worth or that you rarely get to but feel guilty about, and think about, a lot. Cleaning out the garage, making an inventory of all the linens, switching out all the winter clothing that's still in your closet midsummer, or even thinking about your deck that probably has to be replaced in the next few years.

It doesn't have to be forever, but give yourself written permission to not think about or do any of these tasks for a few weeks or months. It will open up time and mental energy for self-care and doing nothing.

Do Nothing While Doing Chores

Yes, doing a chore is doing something, but there are certain chores—the easiest, simplest, most meditative of them—that allow you to put your mind on autopilot. You'll know a chore is ideal for doing nothing because you look forward to it. If the idea of pulling weeds for an hour excites you or you always volunteer to unload the dishwasher because you like that time alone in the kitchen, you already have your do-nothing chores in mind. To make the most of these chores:

- Limit distractions like music, television, or your phone.
- If possible, open a window or take the chore outside if the weather is suitable.
- Perhaps you save chores for later in the evening, when your space is quieter, and that makes it easier to do a chore while in a relaxed, do-nothing state of mind.

If you're not sure which chores will allow you to quiet your mind, test the waters with chores that you normally dread or ones that you find daunting. If there's a chance you can get into the groove of doing a household task on autopilot, with your mind in a calm state, the benefits are manyfold: restorative do-nothing time for yourself and painlessly knocking out some tough tasks. It may not work the first—or even the fifth—time you have to do a particular chore. But as you delight in the positive results from doing nothing, you may find yourself one day slipping into that easy state while doing a chore you once dreaded. The following are some ideas to get you started.

The Perfect Do-Nothing Chores

- **Vacuuming.** Okay, it's loud, but that's a win because no one can talk to you, and you can't hear your phone while you're doing it. Let go of your worries as you suck up those dust bunnies with no one disturbing you.
- **Folding laundry.** Laundry is inevitable, so why not use the time you spend on it to feed your soul? Take that basket of clean clothing to a quiet, screen-free spot—perhaps one with a calming view of the outdoors or a piece of art you've hung up—and fold laundry while you get some joyful do-nothing time in too.
- **Washing dishes.** Turning dishwashing and drying into do-nothing time will actually make you look forward to this chore. Clear your mind, stop thinking about work or what you need to do after the dishes, and put yourself on autopilot. You'll put that last clean pot away and feel refreshed and victorious.
- **Pick up clutter/stuff.** Pick up wayward items and return them to their homes. When you do this in one concentrated time period, instead of separately a hundred times a day, it can be enjoyable and even fun. Make sure to do this activity singularly, without additional fixing or cleaning of items.
- **Wash your car.** Don't get bogged down in details or meticulously vacuuming the inside or wiping down the dashboard. Just dig in to the act of washing the exterior of the car and let your mind clear of distractions as you do this satisfying and simple work.

- **Dusting.** An ideal do-nothing chore, dusting isn't physically taxing and can be stopped and started on a whim. Simply get a dustcloth out and wander your home wiping down surfaces, dusting your mind as you dust your home.

Do-Nothing Rituals for Your Home

Your home is a retreat and a space where you can always find your best self. So, what better place to make doing nothing a steadfast habit in your life? In this section, we will talk about the rituals of home time and how to incorporate doing nothing into them. A ritual is simply a habit or recurring event in your life—it could be as simple as your morning coffee or as expansive as your fifty-person winter holiday get-together.

To get you in the right mind-set, think about the natural flow of your time at home and your existing rituals. You may never have considered it, but you already have a bevy of rituals that you do most days without even thinking or planning for them:

- You awake and do the same stretching ritual or hit the snooze button a certain number of times or jump out of bed and complete your morning routine in the same order: shower, get dressed, pack lunch, breakfast to go, double-check the cat has food and water. Is there such an order to your morning that if you do something out of order, the day gets off track?
- Do you put on the same makeup every day or wear the same tie on Fridays?
- You may even have a small ritual in the parking spot you always take at the office.

No matter what they are, these rituals create an easy calmness to your day. They remove some choice so you can save your decision-making energy for bigger things.

Once you embrace doing nothing, you'll want to make it a ritual in your home alongside all your others. Your do-nothing ritual should:

- Be something you can count on to make your life simpler.
- Make you comfortable, relaxed, and happy.
- Bring you comfort and peace after a difficult day.

Doing nothing can be just as much a part of your routine as brushing your teeth. And just like brushing your teeth, doing nothing gives you an immediate benefit (relaxation, calmness) and long-term benefits from regular practice (mental and physical wellness from stress reduction).

Mealtime Do-Nothing Rituals

Some families and individuals pray before every meal. They always, or almost always, give thanks to their God(s) before they eat. It's easy for them to take this moment of thanks three times a day because it's a ritual that they've built into their life. Mealtimes are a wonderful and regular pause in the day to build your do-nothing ritual around. It could be simple and brief, like shutting your eyes, relaxing your shoulders, and taking a few deep breaths before you dig into your lunch. Or you could end every meal with five minutes of doing nothing, letting your meal digest and clearing your mind before you move on with your day.

You can also make this ritual a family event. This is a great way to introduce doing nothing to children or a spouse. Aim for one meal a day with a quiet pause before or after for doing nothing. Ask one of your family members to lead doing nothing, asking people to put their phones away, turning anything noisy off, and starting and ending the do-nothing time. Don't worry if the pause to do nothing really is just a short minute or two. Even a very brief segment of doing nothing will give everyone the benefit of a clear, calm mind and become a lasting ritual for your family. Here are three ways to bring a do-nothing ritual to mealtimes:

- **Light:** Start dinner with a brief pause of quiet and then ask everyone to share something they're thankful for.
- **Medium:** Make meals a screen-free zone. Distraction-free eating will foster better digestion, and if you're eating with family or friends, better conversation.
- **Deep:** Build your do-nothing time into each meal. Take a pause of five minutes, no matter where you are, to sit quietly and clear your mind. Pairing your do-nothing breaks with mealtimes will ensure you always make this time for yourself.

Do-Nothing Rituals Around Sleep

Most people complain that they don't get enough sleep. We're all busy and often stay up past our optimal bedtime. We like to think of sleep as flexible, getting more when we can and less when we can't. But the truth is, we need sleep like we need air. Good and plentiful sleep is vital to your health. And making a ritual of doing nothing around sleep is a great way to both get better sleep and get more of it. Also, because you have to sleep eventually, this ritual will serve as a friendly reminder to incorporate doing nothing into your day.

At Night

Whatever you choose for a sleep ritual, make it joyful and easy. If you're already doing a lot of sleep hygiene work—no screens for a certain amount of time before bed, quiet calm activities in the late evening—you'll have an easy time making doing nothing a bedtime ritual. If you have busy and unpredictable evenings, work on a twenty-minute bedtime routine that includes your end-of-the-day hygiene and some time to do nothing. Make it very easy to follow and get done: write the few and short steps of the routine on a piece of paper and put it up in your bathroom as a reminder. If that isn't enough, set a few reminders on your phone staggered throughout the evening. You want to remember the routine before you feel so exhausted that you just want to throw yourself into bed and before you get caught up in a stimulating late-night activity. Here are three ideas to make doing nothing part of your evening ritual:

- **Light:** Associate your do-nothing time with a pre-bedtime activity. As in, I put pajamas on and then immediately have a few minutes of quiet to clear my mind or I always take some time to do nothing before I brush my teeth and floss at night.
- **Medium:** Set a curfew for activity in your home. It could be as simple as the television is off, the wireless Internet router is unplugged, and lights are low or off in living areas after ten o'clock. This closing down of home activity can lead everyone to take some quiet do-nothing time before they drift off to sleep.

- **Deep:** Make doing nothing an integral part of your sleep routine. Commit to unwinding most evenings with light and easy screen-free activities that you follow with time to do nothing. Build your do-nothing time up from five minutes to thirty minutes.

In the Morning

Use this same strategy in the morning. Doing nothing after waking up could be as simple as setting two alarms twenty minutes apart. The first one wakes you up. You then sit up in bed, open your curtains, and relax on your bed, enjoying the morning light and the calm and quiet of your environment at this time of day. The more mornings you make this ritual happen, the more you will crave this time to yourself and make it a priority. Here are three ways to make doing nothing part of your morning ritual:

- **Light:** Set your alarm for ten minutes before you need to get up and simply enjoy lying in bed, relaxing, and letting your mind drift. Set a second alarm if you're someone that tends to fall back asleep easily.
- **Medium:** Have silent breakfast a few mornings a week. No radio, no chatter, no cell phone. Just silence with a side of toast.
- **Deep:** Build your morning shower and breakfast routine around a twenty-minute session of doing nothing. Have this restorative and stress-reducing time be a cornerstone of starting your day.

Do-Nothing Rituals When Gathering or Scattering

As you gather, and scatter, you create another pause or transition space to do nothing. If your family always watches a movie together on

Friday evenings, build some do-nothing time in before or after the film. This do-nothing time could be practiced together or just on your own: the anchor is the event already consistently on your family's calendar.

Doing nothing on your own before or after these gatherings also offers many other benefits:

- When you build your do-nothing time around a ritual you already have, a ritual that you do with others and that is consistent, you derive even more enjoyment from that existing ritual. You also ensure you will make the time for doing nothing, just as you make the time for this important event.
- It opens the door to friends and family joining you in your calm and restorative break.
- You're present and engaged in these gatherings, giving everyone your full attention—something that makes them feel valuable, appreciated, and loved—and that feeling you're spreading is contagious. Others see and feel how you are present, alert, and giving of your full attention, and they want to feel that way too. They want to be a positive presence, to fully engage and enjoy the gathering, the activity, and the people, just as you are.

Building your do-nothing time around gathering and scattering can be another positive feedback loop for you in spreading the joy of doing nothing to friends and family. Here are three strategies to incorporating your do-nothing time around gathering and scattering:

- **Light:** After frantically cleaning the bathroom, take a moment for yourself before guests arrive. Even five minutes of quiet and no distractions will put you in the right place mentally to enjoy and engage with your guests.

- **Medium:** Build a buffer of time after the annual soccer tournament to let yourself have some time to decompress.
- **Deep:** Adjust your schedule so you can walk to your twice-weekly basketball practice instead of driving. Use this time and relaxed activity to clear your mind—no listening to podcasts!—and let any stressful thoughts wash away so you can enjoy your time with friends and give your best on the court.

Make Your Entertaining Relaxed and Easy

Everyone needs friendships and community for a healthy and whole life. One way doing nothing can help you build and deepen those friendships and community is by making entertaining and hosting easier. Many of us would love to host people more often, but we get overwhelmed with the work of hosting. Making our home look photo-ready and researching and preparing the perfect meal takes a lot of time and energy. A beautiful benefit of doing nothing is that you see that you don't have to make hosting time-consuming and stressful. You get back to the root of what hosting should be: connecting with people.

The new eyes you have from your practice of doing nothing will allow you to entertain with a new perspective:

- You'll host more often and with less stress.
- You're able to give your friends what they, and you, really want: connection.

- You'll get more comfortable with your home in its regular weekday state—no need to hire a cleaner.
- The meals can be simple and based on whatever is at hand. There's no shame in ordering takeout.

Doing nothing turns your home into a safe and easy space to gather simply by changing how you view hosting: not as a stressful event but rather an easy way to gather with friends. Here are three suggestions for bringing the do-nothing philosophy to your gatherings:

- **Light:** Challenge yourself to invite someone over last minute for dinner. Enjoy the simple pleasure of friendship and company over whatever you've rustled up from the pantry for dinner.
- **Medium:** Invite people over more often for more casual and easy meals or hosting. Think easy drinks on the back porch watching that golden hour of sunlight with a few friends once a week instead of hosting half the neighborhood once a summer for a barbecue complete with a bouncy castle.
- **Deep:** Start an open-door policy with your neighbors. Let them know that you welcome people dropping by unannounced for a friendly chat or to borrow a garden tool or whatever they've run out of for the evening meal.

. . .

As you've seen, bringing the restorative and restful powers of doing nothing into your home life has many rewards. Connect with your roommates, ease the household stress around chores, and find more time for yourself in those fringe hours by doing nothing. You can streamline a few areas of your home to create beautiful spaces to do nothing and deeply relax.

Other Activities

People with many interests live, not only longest, but happiest.
—George Matthew Allen, Newspaper Columnist

As you embrace the philosophy of doing nothing, as you see the power of deep, distraction-free time to yourself, you can also reap those benefits around your other activities, such as hobbies, exercise, volunteering, and socializing (both online and off). Doing nothing will help you engage deeply in your favorite pastimes, streamline your commitments to just those you enjoy most, and give you an extra level of energy for your more challenging pursuits.

Hobbies

Hobbies are a key part of a joyful life. They provide a source of pride and accomplishment. They can be a touchstone to go back to in times of stress. Hobbies can bring a richness to your life, but have you found less and less time for your hobbies lately?

Doing nothing will free you up to rediscover your hobbies. Dig deep and identify one hobby you've put a lot of years and hours into. Are you still in touch with it? If not, why? Think about those passions that you invested years in and how the practice was a comforting ritual. Let doing nothing reintegrate that hobby into your life!

Free Up Time for Hobbies

As you practice doing nothing regularly, you find more time for those hobbies that you've missed. The time you spend deeply relaxing gives back to you more awareness of how you use your time and the motivation to invest yourself in hobbies that you love. You're more comfortable saying no to invitations and asks of your time that don't fit in with your goals or values and that you don't enjoy. This frees up a lot of time as you no longer say yes to things out of guilt, worry that you're missing out, or peer pressure: Your time is your own. You've also learned how to rediscover moments in your day—fringe hours, for example. That time can be split between doing nothing and focusing on your hobby once in a while.

Find More Energy

Where you once said, "I simply don't have the energy in the evening to do_____," you will now have that extra vigor. Because you haven't worn down your body (by not sleeping enough, draining yourself too much at work, or forgetting to take breaks in a busy home life), you have a bit more energy to give than you used to. The rest you give yourself with doing nothing is restorative—not like the "rest" you used to give yourself that involved Netflix, poor posture, and you in a stupor on the couch. It's the kind of rest that gives back to you, helping you unglue yourself from the couch and find that burst of energy to start a game of Scrabble with your spouse or finish up that woodworking project.

Reprioritize Your Hobbies

The distractions you may have lost time to—social media and television—won't have the same draw when you're taking those breaks to do nothing. Your real priorities, the ones that feed your soul, shine through as the things you want to give your time to. When you quiet the chatter around you, you can better see what's important to you. And it might just be early-morning gardening, not checking Snapchat before breakfast. It's also a clarity that you're probably never going to make that quilt, the one that you bought the fabric for three years ago. You're now free to give that fabric away and spend a little more time—guilt free—on the hobbies you do love.

> Doing nothing helps you be more present
> and enjoy the process more.

Better Focus

If you've struggled to get back into a hobby you've taken a break from, doing nothing will help you reconnect. Perhaps you've been deterred by a loss of skills from time off, or it just seems like too much work to get back to that hobby you once loved. Doing nothing helps you be more present and enjoy the process more. You aren't as focused on the results but rather the enjoyment of the action. Being a rusty guitar player or out of practice on your sewing machine doesn't matter: you're simply enjoying the activity.

Plan out your time to take a quick and restorative break to do nothing before you engage in your hobby. Just like with work, a break to do nothing before your hobby helps you let go of distractions and stress. This transitional rest for your body and mind will allow you to get into your hobby with fewer distractions. Doing nothing will be your warm-up to hobby time. You'll already have your phone on silent and be in a place where you can focus without interruption. Doing nothing will have you primed and ready to enjoy one of your life's pleasures.

Streamline

Perhaps doing nothing will lead you to realize that, actually, you *don't* want to spend your time on this hobby anymore. And that's just fine. As you get more connected with your needs and desires by doing nothing, you may find that you've outgrown a hobby. It no longer feeds your soul or brings you the happiness it once did. You can see that other areas of your life are more important to you now.

You now have the tools to peacefully, and without guilt, let that hobby go. (Bonus! You can declutter your home by passing on or selling any tools or equipment you needed to do that hobby.) Doing nothing has tapped into your inner wants and needs and you can now let go of hobbies that don't fit your current life. Your priorities are clearer, and you can finally spend that time you used to spend on your hobby on things that are more pertinent and rewarding to you.

Here are three ways to apply the do-nothing philosophy to your hobbies:

- **Light:** Use your new energy from doing nothing to reconnect once a week with an old hobby, one you've been saying for years that you want to get back to.
- **Medium:** Take your favorite hobby to the next level, registering for an advanced course, signing up for an open mic, or joining a league team. The bravery and time will come from embracing the do-nothing philosophy.
- **Deep:** Let go of an old hobby that doesn't fit in with your life anymore. Sell those skis while you're in a season of having young kids and just don't have the time to get to the mountains. Take this brave step with the Zen you get from doing nothing: someday it may be the right hobby for you again, but it's not today.

Doing Nothing on Social Media

One of the hobbies that takes up precious time on a daily basis is checking social media. Nowadays, everyone uses it for pleasure (to catch up on friends' lives), for family information (to find out that a child's track meet was canceled), and for career purposes (connecting with colleagues on LinkedIn). These are important aspects of your life, so it's not realistic to imagine you swearing off social media forever. Instead, you can learn how to incorporate it into your life in a balanced way that still gives you time to do nothing. In this section, we will examine all the ways social media usage can enhance or hinder your time to do nothing and also how you can spread the word about doing nothing through social media if you choose to.

Try to keep your mind open with these next suggestions. Most of us will find cutting back on social media to be a challenging exercise.

Keep a vision of yourself doing one of your most enjoyable and relaxing do-nothing activities at the forefront of your thoughts to help boost your motivation. You'll simply be making some small changes to give yourself more space for resetting and relaxing. You're taking a break from sharing a new purchase, a killer view, or a beautifully tiled floor with your friends...and instead, you're sharing a photo or sentence about joyfully doing nothing. You're encouraging and including friends in plans to be highly unproductive. You're helping them see that doing nothing should be celebrated and embraced regularly. Unclench your shoulders, put your feet up on the coffee table, and let's start.

Take Back Some Social Media Time for Doing Nothing

Social media can be a slippery slope. A few passes through Snapchat, Instagram, text messages, and your email, and your time for doing nothing has turned into "kind of doing something but not really doing a lot." Phones and our social media accounts are omnipresent in today's life. We think of them as helpful, or even benign, but they can command your time and focus without you making a conscious decision to give them anything. If you're struggling to find time in your day for some joyful do-nothingness, take a look at how much time you're spending flipping through your social media accounts. Are you someone who checks in once a day? Do you leave your phone on silent for long stretches and only return messages when you consciously decide to open your phone? Are you vigilant about putting your phone away during family meals and while hanging out with friends? If so, you're probably on a good path to keeping your social media usage in check. If, however, you checked your Instagram and Facebook accounts in between those last few sentences, let's talk. There is work to be done.

> If you're struggling to find time in your day for some joyful do-nothingness, take a look at how much time you're spending flipping through your social media accounts.

Your do-nothing time is a perfect way to reassess your social media usage. The two are inherently at odds with each other—you can't truly find self-care in your do-nothing time if you're on social media because:

- Social media is about connecting—you want to *disconnect* to make the most of your do-nothing time.
- Social media is also about seeing and being seen. You want to make your do-nothing time personal. It doesn't need to be shared in the moment. Sure, take a picture of yourself doing nothing if you really feel inspired, but that's it. Save the picture to enjoy later or maybe even share in a few days.
- You don't want to make that time about someone else by looking through someone else's photos or updates about their life.

If you struggle with checking your phone and accounts frequently, start with a simple challenge to keep it tucked away for an hour or two one day a week and build from there. Challenge yourself to leave your phone at home for short errands. If your do-nothing activity is outside, try leaving your phone at home while you pick wildflowers or people-watch from a park bench. Pulling back a bit from social media will allow you to enjoy the full benefit of aimlessly and joyfully doing nothing. Here are three ways to go about it:

- **Light:** Put your phone on a charger at nine o'clock every night—as far away from your bed as possible.
- **Medium:** Take a day offline once a week. Accept phone calls, but everything else—text messages, social media accounts, email—goes unread and unanswered until the next day.
- **Deep:** Go analog. That's right: toss your smartphone. Get an older model, non-smartphone phone. You'll save a ton of cash and even more time.

Scale Back the Number of Accounts You Maintain

Do you really need to post that photo of the seagull that stole your bratwurst out of your hand to multiple channels? You don't need to share everything in every possible way all the time. Sharing the same photo via group text, Snapchat, Twitter, Instagram, and Facebook is a time suck. Responding to every comment you get in each of those places is even more of a time suck. One way to make things simple and find more time for doing nothing is to streamline your social media accounts.

To start, focus your social media time and energy only on your most-used and enjoyed channels. We all start from different places on this, so do what's right for you. Some of us may start with cutting down from six different social media accounts to four and others may stream-line to just one account or even none. If you're a fervent social media user and can't bear to part with any account, consider using a social media management platform that posts the same update or photo to all of your accounts. From there, choose the platform with the highest engagement to respond and like other posts on. Baby steps.

One way to make things simple and find more time for doing nothing is to streamline your social media accounts.

If it scares you to shut down or delete an account, just put it on pause. Or test the waters by deleting the app on your phone before shutting an account down. Remember that you are doing this to give yourself more time to do nothing and to make it easier for you to go offline while doing nothing. Give yourself short-term and easy goals, like removing one app from your phone for just a day and then aiming for another day. When it gets easier, remove another app or take the plunge and delete an account.

Most important, take notice of how these changes affect your life. How does it feel to have fewer accounts or to be checking your accounts less often? Do you really feel you are missing out? Do you notice you have a bit more time? Do you notice that with a smaller stream of news-feeds from friends and family that you have more peace and more time to spend on yourself, doing nothing when you please and with background noise to ignore? Start slowly and let the enjoyment of less social media time build in your life. Here are three ways to cut back on your social media accounts:

- **Light:** Remove one or two social media apps from your phone to reduce the time you spend on them.
- **Medium:** Close half of your social media accounts.
- **Deep:** Tell your friends you can only be contacted via email or text.

Redefine Your Status Updates

Finding the joy in doing nothing is not only healing and meditative, it's also an act of rebellion. Claiming your time to do nothing is a bold and countercultural action in this time where busyness is celebrated as a virtue. What better way to share your newfound joy in unproductive afternoons than on your social media streams? Dare yourself to share one of your do-nothing activities. And share it not in an ironic or self-deprecating way, but share it from a perspective of appreciation. Share it unfiltered. As we've talked about, doing nothing with great joy is only for those lucky enough to have the time and privilege to do so. So, share a real photo of yourself, bare bones, unlit, doing nothing extreme or exotic or exclusive. Tell your friends that yes, you are doing nothing and you're thankful for it. Share that there is truth and beauty in our poorly lit and mismatched color-paletted lives. Share that you can appreciate these moments, the ones that may look ugly to others, just as much as you appreciate the beautiful and edited ones. Here are three ways to go about it:

- **Light:** Share a status update of "Doing nothing and thankful for it."
- **Medium:** Show off your "real" lunch of a protein bar and leftover pad thai eaten cold out of the box.
- **Deep:** Share a one-minute video of you doing nothing.

Reduce the Online White Noise in Your Day to Do Nothing

Something that trips up even the most focused and earnest in their plans to kick back and be as thoroughly unproductive and disconnected as possible: the white noise of modern life. It's a constant in most of our lives—the online chatter, the noise of mobile phones ringing, the compulsion to check that one thing on your phone when you're at the movies, plus the visual noise around us of billboards, newspaper advertisements, and pop-up ads on your favorite news aggregate sites. We're so used to this constant, in-your-face entertainment, advertisement, and noise assault that we don't even notice if we're adding to it. We don't leave our home without earbuds in and a podcast on. We don't dare sit down at a restaurant without an app open on our phone. We can't sit in a doctor's office waiting room without searching for even more distraction. We are hooked on the white noise of life.

This constant background chatter makes it difficult to peacefully and singularly do nothing. We are so accustomed to constantly hearing things and checking things that it can feel uncomfortable and even strange not to. Sitting in silence is almost unheard of these days unless you're in the final ten-minute meditation of your hatha yoga class. But you can do it. And there are some easy ways to start that do not involve living with blinders on or throwing away your cell phone.

Ways to Reduce the White Noise in Your Life

- Put your phone on Do Not Disturb. Try to set some "sleep" hours for your phone, just like you do for yourself.

- Leave the television/podcast/radio/music off. If you automatically turn something on when you're home, something to fill the room and entertain you while you do other things, turn it off. Spend some time in silence with your thoughts.
- Go somewhere really quiet. If you're a city dweller, you may not realize how much noise and distraction is in your day-to-day life. Find a silent space, be it your parent's basement or a short trip outside the city to a forest.
- Turn off most notifications on your phone. Do you really need that app for your favorite NHL team notifying you about player trades the minute they happen?
- Go ad-free in your television viewing. Ditch the cable and just use streaming services that have no advertisements. Not seeing those ads will give you back some mental real estate and soothe your brain.

Here are different levels you can aim for to cut out the white noise:

- **Light:** Trade your earbuds and podcasts on your morning commute for deep silence from noise-cancelation headphones.
- **Medium:** Liberally use the Do Not Disturb function on your phone when working and doing nothing. Remember: true emergencies, the life-or-death kind, are very rare. Seeing a funny GIF in your WhatsApp chat three hours after everyone else did is not an emergency.
- **Deep:** Take a day of silence once a month. Go offline and retreat to the woods to commune with nature in silence from sunup until sundown.

Exercise

Exercising is another popular hobby that you probably want to fit into your schedule. Doing nothing can give you that extra boost to start a new exercise program or take your current one to another level. You've learned how the restorative power of doing nothing helps you engage and excel at work: it can do the same thing with exercise. You're more engaged, you make the time for things that are truly important to you, and you have the energy to do your best at them. The power of doing nothing can be a catalyst for so much great change in your life, and exercise is no exception.

Find the Motivation to Go

Have you ever put your gym clothes on and then...just sat there? You intended to go to the gym or out for a run, you really wanted to make it happen, but you let yourself get distracted by a few things. After a few spins around your social media channels or deciding now was the time to clean out your refrigerator, the motivation to get your sweat on disappeared. This common hurdle to creating an exercise habit, one you never skip, can be cured with doing nothing. Here's how:

1. Put your exercise clothing on.
2. Take five minutes to do nothing. Find a quiet spot, turn your phone off, and relax.
3. Release any thoughts of work or home life and simply do nothing.

You'll emerge from this restorative break with resolve and excitement for your workout. Without any distractions to waylay you, you'll head right out to the gym and get a hard but enjoyable workout. You'll start to see the positive results from quality, consistent exercise that you've always wanted. This positive feedback loop of doing nothing, having a great workout, and seeing the results you're after, inculcates the habit of exercise in your life. You'll stop abandoning workouts before you even get to the gym when you make a habit of doing nothing beforehand.

Get More Out of Your Workouts

Relaxation techniques, visualization, and meditation are part of a holistic approach to performance that many professional and amateur athletes subscribe to. The ability to quickly calm yourself and stay focused in a stressful situation is paramount to athletic success. Doing nothing helps you develop a deeper level of focus.

This deeper level of focus translates to maximizing your performance. No more phoning it in: you're engaged, present, and able to push through old barriers to improve technique and gain endurance. The runner finds that next gear and runs that last mile faster than the first. The yoga enthusiast finally masters a pose they've been stuck on for months. They're able to block out distractions and up their fitness using skills gleaned from doing nothing.

Find That Do-Nothing Time As Part of Your Exercise Routine

Doing nothing can not only improve your exercise routine, but it can also be a part of it. You can connect the exercise you schedule into your day to doing nothing by adding a period of doing nothing before or after your workout:

- The break *before* will help you reset and get focused for your workout.
- A break to do nothing *after* exercise will help center you as you transition to your next activity.

For example, enter that gym ten minutes before your boot camp class starts and sit in the corner, take a few deep breaths, and keep your gaze soft as you let your stress melt away and your mind clear. Use the pre-run stretch time with your running group to steal some quiet and feel the present and peaceful state of doing nothing. Lots of people have pre-exercise rituals around hydration, stretching, checking their phone, or starting their warm-up. Make doing nothing part of your own warm-up routine.

Learn to Love Exercise

If exercising isn't your favorite part of your day, doing nothing can help make it more enjoyable.

Find Focus

One obstacle to enjoying exercise is being distracted or finding it hard to engage with what you're doing. Maybe your mind is wandering and all you can think about is how uncomfortable you are, how much time is left, and all the other things you'd rather be doing. Doing nothing before you exercise will help you focus. You'll be more in the moment when you exercise and reflect on the feel-good aspects of it, how your muscles feel awake, your body is invigorated, and you're so homed in on what you're doing, you can't give any mental real estate to outside thoughts and distractions.

Choose an Activity That's Right for You

Doing nothing will give you the confidence to focus on an activity that fits your personality and lifestyle. If a traditional gym membership or running club has never been a good fit, if you tried all the classes your friends raved about—hot yoga, barre, CrossFit—and never enjoyed any of them, doing nothing can open you up to different forms of exercise. Maybe you really love walking everywhere and instead of forcing yourself to ride the stationary bike three times a week, you instead leave your car at home twice a week and walk both ways to work. Or maybe you've always wanted to learn to dance hip-hop or even ballet, and you start taking adult dance classes. Or maybe you just really love cleaning, so you decide to make that your exercise, putting some ankle weights on and getting your sweat on while you scrub the tile in your shower. Doing nothing brings your real desires and joys to the surface and makes it easier to recognize those things that you, not your friends or coworkers or family, really enjoy.

Enjoy the Process

Doing nothing can get you centered on being process-driven in your exercise. Sometimes we get too focused on the goal, and all we can think about is when the activity will be over or how much we have to do to achieve our goal. We are thinking about the end result instead of thinking about the act that gets us there. Doing nothing, being present, allows us to embrace the process of exercise. We can enjoy the sights, sounds, and feelings during our run instead of checking our watch every two minutes and thinking about when it will be over. You can let yourself get obsessed with the joy in your exercise instead of constantly thinking about the results you want from it. And the irony: being process-driven will not only help you enjoy your exercise more, but it can also get us the results we want faster.

Doing nothing, being present, allows us to embrace the process of exercise.

Here are three ways to incorporate the do-nothing philosophy in your exercise program:

- **Light:** Find your favorite exercise regime. As you take breaks to do nothing and get more in tune with your body and mind, figure out what the perfect mix of exercise is for you. Use those cues from your body and mind to take rest days or push harder or switch up your routine.
- **Medium:** Appreciate your body when you do nothing. Come out of that centered and calm time and think thankful and positive thoughts for your body that is gliding you through a dance class, marching you along on a charity walk, or letting you dominate in your age category at a tennis tournament.
- **Deep:** Use the practice of doing nothing to take your performance to the next level. If you're a cyclist or runner or yoga practitioner, use doing nothing before you practice or compete to center yourself and bring a clear and focused mind to the workout or race.

Volunteering and Social Activism

The practice of doing nothing gives you more clarity about what's important in your life and what you want to give your time and energy to. As you find yourself reshaping how you spend your time, you may rethink how much time you want to give to volunteer activities and causes. That time spent quietly doing nothing has a way of making you see so clearly those things that truly matter to you and that you want to give yourself to. The mindfulness that comes from doing nothing will open up your mind and help you reshape how you give your time and dollars to your favorite causes.

It's exciting to think about the far-reaching effects of your choice to do nothing. This simple tool to relax and de-stress could lead you to doing more good than you ever believed possible. You could start volunteering for the first time or even donate a percentage of your income to a cause you feel strongly about. However you support your favorite charity or organization, the returns of connection, feeling helpful, and doing good will be exponential.

Find the Energy and Time to Give

If you've always wanted to volunteer but have struggled to find the time, doing nothing can give you that entry point. Once you've made a habit of doing nothing in your evenings, shutting off your phone and the television for deep relaxation, those evening hours are now open to so many possibilities. One of those things could be volunteering. You're no longer intimidated by the idea of blocking off one night a week to help out at a local shelter or to stuff envelopes or to tutor kids in your neighborhood. The time has actually been there all along—you just needed to see what it could really be used for. Doing nothing gives you that.

You not only find that you have more time to give than you thought, but you also now have more energy. Those restorative breaks to do nothing keep you humming along all day and pick you up out of any energy lows. If volunteering your time wasn't possible because you simply had no extra energy to give, you've got a new way to energize yourself. Doing nothing can give you a boost, help you shake off any of the stress of your work or other activities that tend to drain you. You've got a way to restart yourself, and that means you can give three hours a week to something meaningful that's a delight to you instead of a chore. You'll probably even find that giving back gives back to you. You'll feel happier, more fulfilled, and more connected to the people around you.

Find New Ways to Give That Matter to You

Connecting with yourself can also unearth the causes and work that matter to you most. Just like with doing nothing in conjunction with your work, you may find a new spark for a cause through these quiet and restorative breaks. Run with it. Enjoy that you have a passion and a cause that you're ready to give yourself to. It could be serving at your church, a community organization, your child's school, or an international aid group. Whatever it is, you can open yourself to it when you do nothing.

Through doing nothing, you can also spark new ideas for ways to give. It may not just be giving money or your time. For example:

- Perhaps you have other professional skills you can give an organization for free.
- Maybe you have something of use, like extra room to host guests of the organization or you own a vehicle you could loan out for the work of the organization.
- You might have an everyday skill that's useful—cooking a meal for someone recovering from a surgery or shoveling an elderly neighbor's driveway.

You can make these beautiful connections when your mind gets rebooted regularly through doing nothing.

Let Go If It Doesn't Engage You

Doing nothing can also be the path to seeing that your heart just isn't into a particular cause you have been supporting, either in dollars or in time. You may have either grown apart from the work or the mandate of the organization, or it could have grown apart from you. There is no shame in admitting this. As you take the time to "fill the well" by doing nothing, you'll connect with the things that you can really give to and enjoy.

So, let go of the cause or volunteering that you are struggling to connect with. Doing good should feel good too. As you make more time to do nothing, you will gain some clarity around what cause or organization matters to you now. You will find that your inner philanthropist has time and skills or money to happily invest in the kind of doing good that feeds your soul.

Give Up Some of Your Wants
to Support Things You Love

Just as doing nothing gives you new eyes for how much time you can dedicate to a cause, it also gives you a new perspective on how you can financially support causes you love. When you take the time to deeply relax, you see that some of your wants are just that, wants—not needs. Since doing nothing helps you curb your casual spending—because you feel more fulfilled by the simple pleasures of life—you can then devote more of your budget to helping others. You can engage in philanthropy, big and small, when you give up some of your extras that you won't even miss.

Think of financial giving as a true luxury. To be able to give money away is often thought of as something just the rich can do. But even people with modest incomes can donate financially to their beloved causes. And it's another positive feedback loop: you see you don't really need some of your extras, you donate to a great cause, and you feel so good about your philanthropy that you cut a few more extras so you can give more. When you take that time to do nothing, a form of luxurious self-care that doesn't cost a penny, you find that your needs in this life are simple.

When you take that time to do nothing, a form of luxurious self-care that doesn't cost a penny, you find that your needs in this life are simple.

A life of simple pleasures allows you to give to those causes most dear to you. Here are three ways to use the do-nothing philosophy when it comes to volunteering:

- **Light:** Volunteer for the first time at an event. Use the calming effect of doing nothing to get over any fears you may have and sign up to support an athletic, cultural, or civic event.
- **Medium:** Unearth what cause(s) really matter to you. Is it supporting research for a disease that's affected your family or a community organization that had a deep influence on you growing up? Whatever it is, use that time after your do-nothing break when you're free from mental clutter to do some soul-searching about what causes mean the most to you.
- **Deep:** Set a lifetime philanthropy goal. It could be a percentage of your income or a match to something in your life, like the cost of your home, what you spent on your wedding, or a year's salary. Tracking your giving beyond your annual tax return will be a fun, motivating, and positive hobby.

Save Money When You Do Nothing

Doing nothing is accessible to everyone, not only because you can do it almost anywhere at any time but also because it's free. So many similar wellness plans ask you to open your wallet for a gym membership, classes, or expensive supplements. There's no need to call for an appointment or get just some of the cost reimbursed through your health plan. Isn't it wonderful to find something *free* that so positively impacts your life and wellness?

It's not just a free activity, either. Doing nothing helps you spend less and save more in many other ways too:

- You open your eyes to the simple (and cheap!) pleasures in your life when you do nothing.
- You are less stressed and therefore less susceptible to impulse purchases.
- You really see what you need when you do nothing, and that helps you have fewer wants. (Wants can be very expensive!)
- Quick, simple, and healthy meals at home start to win out over expensive and unhealthy dining out. You think, "Why would I spend all that money and not feel very good after the meal when I could easily and cheaply eat something delicious at home?"
- You start to appreciate those simple, easy, and free options, and they become your default. An evening stroll with friends wins out over expensive concert tickets.
- Hosting people simply and casually, being able to have great conversations over a leisurely evening, wins out over noisy, crowded, and expensive restaurants.
- You give up that expensive cable package because your evenings are filled with other things now: doing nothing, reading books from the library, and spending quality time with family and friends. Doing nothing has opened you to the sweet, simple, and mostly free pleasures in your life.
- What makes you happy becomes clear when you do nothing. And you see that you can't really buy happiness. So, wandering a store looking for a pick-me-up or thinking that buying some big-ticket item, like a new car or a renovated kitchen, will make you happy is

no longer part of your life philosophy. You know what makes you happy, and it's simple, mostly free things like time to relax, doing great work, and connecting with people you love.

- It becomes clear that you already have what you need when you take breaks to do nothing. When shelter and food—the basics—are covered and we're relaxed and less stressed, our wants can clearly be separated from our needs. When we easily see those wants for what they are, nice things that won't actually make us any happier or improve our life, we can say no to them.

In our fast-paced world, it's easy to think of wants as needs: *I need a new phone* or *I need an expensive vacation*. We're often busy looking at what others have, getting distracted by their pursuit of wants, instead of staying focused on the things that we have and that fulfill us. Doing nothing brings you back to that center and helps remove any urgency from your wants. Sure, those things would be nice, but they're not worth it if they come at the expense of other things like time for self-care, our friends, and our long-term goals.

> Doing nothing brings you back to that center and helps remove any urgency from your wants.

You remove negative influences on your spending when you do nothing. Here are three ideas for using the do-nothing philosophy to spend less:

- **Light:** Have a "no spend day" once a month. This is a day when you make every effort to buy nothing: outside of train fare for your commute to work or a recurring bill that comes out of your checking account, don't spend anything. Enjoy everything you already have: food in your kitchen, clothes you already own, and entertainment that's free.
- **Medium:** Set a goal to bump your monthly savings by 10 percent and use doing nothing as your tool. Change one of your expensive activities into a time to do nothing and practice frugality in one of the areas you struggle with, like dining out or buying new electronics.
- **Deep:** Cut up your credit cards and move to a cash-spending system. If you struggle with using credit, moving to a cash-only system will make you hyper-aware of your spending and bring lots of motivation to stick to purchasing just what you need.

Take the Do-Nothing Pause Before Spending

Taking a break to do nothing can also serve as a physical pause before shopping or deciding to make a big purchase. If you struggle with impulse purchases or you're trying to stick to a budget, doing nothing can be a great tool to prevent yourself from spending on things you don't need. Simply take five minutes to pause and clear your mind before you enter a store. If you're already shopping, step out of the store, clear your mind, and take a deep, distraction-free break to relax. As you come out of your time doing nothing, you'll not only have deeper willpower to resist spending, but you will also be able to analyze the purchase without emotion. You won't have stress or guilt or boredom driving how you spend your money.

• • •

As you can see, doing nothing can have a positive effect in many areas of your life. It can be a tool to live more deeply and consciously in so many ways. Whether it's exercise, hobbies, social media, spending, or volunteering, you can reshape your habits and activities with the power of doing nothing. The fresh eyes you get from this deeply relaxing break show you exactly what really matters to you, what brings you joy, and what feeds your soul.

You're Ready to Joyfully Do Nothing Now

Doing nothing is a gateway to productivity, peace, and joy. Kicking back and deeply relaxing—which you earn and deserve—actually help you enjoy your life more and find success. The time you put into doing nothing, a deep and restful relaxation you probably don't often treat yourself to, pays you back in many ways.

Deep Rest Is Vital for Wellness

That restful and plentiful sleep, the lowered stress levels, the boost of energy, the creative spark—it can all be found with regular practice of doing nothing. When you take this restorative pause, you not only lower your stress levels (an important step in general wellness), but you also give yourself the motivation and focus to invest in other areas of wellness: eating nourishing food, getting more movement in your day, and enjoying your precious sleep. Doing nothing sparks an investment and commitment to wellness in all areas.

Doing Nothing Helps You Do More

Do nothing to do...something. As you've read, restorative breaks to do nothing make you a more focused employee, partner, friend, and parent. Doing nothing helps you do that hard work—the kind of work that we often struggle with finding the focus and motivation for. You get energy from breaks to do nothing—the kind of energy you don't get from a "regular" break where your mind is still busy and you're distracted. After a break to do nothing, the innovative ideas come. You can tackle tough work easily. You can give it your all because you just took that deeply restful time to do nothing.

Doing nothing also clarifies what work is important and what work isn't important. You cut down the amount of work in front of you after taking these joyful breaks to do nothing. You boil it down to the meaningful and the essential. You're able to prioritize and don't lose time on projects that suck up your energy without results. A break to do nothing actually gives you back time, helping you do better work faster.

Have Less White Noise in Your Life

There are so many fun and different ways to stay connected at all times these days, but sometimes it's hard to turn off that information stream. When you do nothing, you turn off that white noise—that constant connection and the streams of information. You carve out your own mental space for quiet and let your brain reboot. Just as your computer can get bogged down with too many programs and applications running, so can your brain. Your mind can get cluttered when you don't take time to regularly relax and shut out the constant stream of information. You start to focus on things that don't really matter to you, don't impact you positively, and aren't giving back to you in a meaningful way. Doing nothing restarts your mind, setting it back to its natural aware and focused state. It brings you back to your core beliefs and values and back to the people and things that really matter to you.

> Doing nothing restarts your mind, setting it back to its
> natural aware and focused state.

Doing nothing also trains you to weed out the nonessential information. When you take that time for quiet and shutting out the worries or random thoughts, you beef up your ability to listen for the essential among all the chatter out there. You can then translate this to other areas of your life, streamlining your newsfeeds and social media streams to just your favorites and putting more time toward those things and people that matter to you.

Get More of What You Love

Instead of that nagging feeling of things you "have to do" or things you're "supposed to do" or the uneasy feeling that you're not getting everything that you need to done, you come out of your time joyfully doing nothing...

- **With a fresh blank canvas.** You add things back in that are a true priority and that you really enjoy.
- **Rested and reminded of what you enjoy most.** It could be an activity or a person. It could even be more time for doing nothing, undisturbed by anyone or any thought, that you want more of in your life.

Doing nothing is a way to start fresh and prioritize what's important to you.

Start Doing Nothing...Right Now!

You've read about how to do nothing and why to do nothing. You've heard about the benefits, how this short, sweet, simple activity can bring wellness, focus, and more good into your life. So now, do nothing! Put this book down, remove or turn off any distractions, and go sit on your patio or look out the window for ten minutes. Let any thoughts or worries lift from you. Take a few deep breaths, relax your shoulders, and joyfully do nothing.

Sources

Arnold, Jeanne E., Anthony P. Graesch, Enzo Ragazzini, and Elinor Ochs. *Life at Home in the Twenty-First Century: 32 Families Open Their Doors* (The Cotsen Institute of Archaeology Press, 2012)

CareerBuilder. "New CareerBuilder Survey Reveals How Much Smartphones Are Sapping Productivity at Work," www.prnewswire.com/news-releases/new-careerbuilder-survey-reveals-how-much-smartphones-are-sapping-productivity-at-work-300281718.html

Dartmouth Student Wellness Center. "Relaxation, Stress & Sleep," www.dartmouth.edu/~healthed/relax/

Hannon, Kerry. *Love Your Job: The New Rules for Career Happiness* (John Wiley & Sons, Inc., 2015)

Hanscom, Angela J. *Balanced and Barefoot: How Unrestricted Outdoor Play Makes for Strong, Confident, and Capable Children* (New Harbinger Publications, 2016)

J.J. Keller & Associates. "DOT Hours of Service Rules–FAQs," www.jjkeller.com/learn/hours-of-service-faqs

Mayo Clinic. "Relaxation techniques: Try these steps to reduce stress," www.mayoclinic.org/healthy-lifestyle/stress-management/in-depth/relaxation-technique/art-20045368

McMains, Stephanie and Sabine Kastner. "Interactions of Top-Down and Bottom-Up Mechanisms in Human Visual Cortex," www.jneurosci.org/content/31/2/587.full

Mitchell, Heidi. "Taking the Right Kind of Break Makes You a Better Worker," www.wsj.com/articles/taking-the-right-kind-of-break-makes-you-a-better-worker-1494986521

Nauert, Rick, PhD. "Taking Breaks Found to Improve Attention," https://psychcentral.com/news/2011/02/09/taking-breaks-found-to-improve-attention/23329.html

Pallarito, Karen. "Why Taking a Break at Work Makes You a Better Employee," www.health.com/home/workday-breaks-help-employees-reboot-researchers-say

Perry, Mark J. "New US homes today are 1,000 square feet larger than in 1973 and living space per person has nearly doubled," www.aei.org/publication/new-us-homes-today-are-1000-square-feet-larger-than-in-1973-and-living-space-per-person-has-nearly-doubled/

Salleh, Mohamed Razali. "Life Event, Stress and Illness," www.ncbi.nlm.nih.gov/pmc/articles/PMC3341916/

Schwartz, Tony. "Relax! You'll Be More Productive," www.nytimes.com/2013/02/10/opinion/sunday/relax-youll-be-more-productive.html

Steakley, Lia. "Optimizing work breaks for health, job satisfaction and productivity," http://scopeblog.stanford.edu/2015/09/11/optimizing-work-breaks-for-health-job-satisfaction-and-productivity/

Sydney Morning Herald. "Relax—it's good for you," www.smh.com.au/lifestyle/relax--its-good-for-you-20090819-eqlo.html

Thompson, Derek. "A Formula for Perfect Productivity: Work for 52 Minutes, Break for 17," www.theatlantic.com/business/archive/2014/09/science-tells-you-how-many-minutes-should-you-take-a-break-for-work-17/380369/

White, Aimee. "Anxiety Coping Strategy: The Benefits of Relaxation," www.healthyplace.com/blogs/anxietypanic/2010/02/anxiety-tool-the-benefits-of-relaxation/

Woodrow Wilson School. "Two WWS professors release new study, 'Income's influence on happiness,'" wws.princeton.edu/news-and-events/news/item/two-wws-professors-release-new-study-income's-influence-happiness

About the Author

Rachel Jonat is the author of *Do Less: A Minimalist Guide to a Simplified, Organized, and Happy Life* (Adams Media, 2014) and *The Minimalist Mom: How to Simply Parent Your Baby* (Adams Media, 2016). A sought-out expert on minimalism and simplifying, she has been featured on television and radio, *The Globe and Mail* (Toronto), Babble.com, and *Business Insider*. She lives in Vancouver, Canada, with her husband and three sons. You can read more of her work at her popular blog TheMinimalistMom.com.